WITHDRAWN

REGENTS RESTORATION DRAMA SERIES

General Editor: John Loftis

THE PROVOKED HUSBAND

SIR JOHN VANBRUGH

and

COLLEY CIBBER

The Provoked Husband

Edited by

PETER DIXON

UNIVERSITY OF NEBRASKA PRESS · LINCOLN

MANUFACTURED IN THE UNITED STATES OF AMERICA

Regents Restoration Drama Series

The Regents Restoration Drama Series provides soundly edited texts, in modern spelling, of the more significant plays of the late seventeenth and early eighteenth centuries. The word "Restoration" is here used ambiguously and must be explained. A strict definition of the word would be unacceptable to everyone, for it would exclude, among many other plays, those of Congreve. If to the historian it refers to the period between 1660 and 1685 (or 1688), it has long been used by the student of drama in default of a more precise term to refer to plays belonging to the dramatic tradition established in the 1660s, weakening after 1700, and displaced in the 1730s. It is in this extended sense— imprecise though justified by academic custom—that the word is used in this series, which includes plays first produced between 1660 and 1737. Although these limiting dates are determined by political events, the return of Charles II (and the removal of prohibitions against operation of theaters) and the passage of Walpole's Stage Licensing Act, they enclose a period of dramatic history having a coherence of its own in the establishment, development, and disintegration of a tradition.

The editors have planned the series with attention to the projected dimensions of the completed whole, a representative collection of Restoration drama providing a record of artistic achievement and providing also a record of the deepest concerns of three generations of Englishmen. And thus it contains deservedly famous plays—*The Country Wife*, *The Man of Mode*, and *The Way of the World*—and also significant but little known plays, *The Virtuoso*, for example, and *City Politiques*, the former a satirical review of scientific investigation in the early years of the Royal Society, the latter an equally satirical review of politics at the time of the Popish Plot. If the volumes of famous plays finally achieve the larger circulation, the other volumes may have the greater utility, in making available texts otherwise difficult of access with the editorial apparatus needed to make them intelligible.

The editors have had the instructive example of the parallel and senior project, the Regents Renaissance Drama Series; they have in fact used the editorial policies developed for the earlier plays as their own, modifying them as appropriate for the later period and as the experience of successive editions suggested. The introductions to the separate Restoration plays differ considerably in their nature. Although a uniform body of relevant information is presented in each of them, no attempt has been made to impose a pattern of interpretation. Emphasis in the introductions has necessarily varied with the nature of the plays and inevitably—we think desirably—with the special interests and aptitudes of the different editors.

Each text in the series is based on a fresh collation of the seventeenth- and eighteenth-century editions that might be presumed to have authority. The textual notes, which appear above the rule at the bottom of each page, record all substantive departures from the edition used as the copy-text. Variant substantive readings among contemporary editions are listed there as well. Editions later than the eighteenth century are referred to in the textual notes only when an emendation originating in some one of them is received into the text. Variants of accidentals (spelling, punctuation, capitalization) are not recorded in the notes except in instances in which they have, or may have, substantive relevance. Contracted forms of characters' names are silently expanded in speech prefixes and stage directions and, in the case of speech prefixes, are regularized. Additions to the stage directions of the copy-text are enclosed in brackets.

Spelling has been modernized along consciously conservative lines, but within the limits of a modernized text the linguistic quality of the original has been carefully preserved. Contracted preterites have regularly been expanded. Punctuation has been brought into accord with modern practices. The objective has been to achieve a balance between the pointing of the old editions and a system of punctuation which, without overloading the text with exclamation marks, semicolons, and dashes, will make the often loosely flowing verse and prose of the original syntactically intelligible to the modern reader. Dashes are regularly used only to indicate interrupted speeches, or shifts of address within a single speech.

Explanatory notes, chiefly concerned with glossing obsolete words and phrases, are printed below the textual notes at the bottom of each page. References to stage directions in the notes follow the admirable system of the Revels editions, whereby stage directions are keyed, decimally, to the line of the text before or after which they occur. Thus, a note on 0.2 has reference to the second line of the stage direction at the beginning of the scene in question. A note on 115.1 has reference to the first line of the stage direction following line 115 of the text of the relevant scene. Speech prefixes, and any stage directions attached to them, are keyed to the first line of accompanying dialogue.

JOHN LOFTIS

Stanford University

Contents

List of Abbreviations

O1	Octavo, 1728, first edition ([x] + 99 + [ii] pages).
O2	Octavo, 1728 ([x] + 95 + [ii] pages).
O3	Octavo, 1729, "The Second Edition."
1730	Sir John Vanbrugh. *Plays*. 2 vols. 1730.
1735	Duodecimo, 1735.
Apology	*An Apology for the Life of Colley Cibber . . . Written by Himself.* Ed. B. R. S. Fone. Ann Arbor, 1968.
Mrs. Delany	*The Autobiography and Correspondence of Mary Granville, Mrs. Delany.* Ed. Lady Llanover. 3 vols. London, 1861.
Provoked Wife	Sir John Vanbrugh. *The Provoked Wife*. Ed. Curt A. Zimansky. Lincoln, Nebraska, 1969.
OED	*Oxford English Dictionary*
om.	omitted
Seymour	Richard Seymour. *The Compleat Gamester: in Three Parts.* 5th edn. London, 1734.
S.D.	stage direction

Introduction

For our knowledge of the genesis of *The Provoked Husband* we are almost entirely dependent on Cibber's Preface and Prologue to the play. From these we learn that during the last years of his life Vanbrugh was working on a new comedy entitled *A Journey to London*. Shortly before his death in 1726 he discussed its plan and structure with Cibber, into whose hands the unfinished manuscript subsequently passed, and from whose hands it emerged two years later as a "regular" five-act play. Its new title looks back to Vanbrugh's youthful success, *The Provoked Wife*, even while it affirms that Cibber has set his own stamp on the work, characteristically giving prominence to the scenes of domestic strife in high society. *The Provoked Husband; or, a Journey to London* opened at Drury Lane on January 10, 1728. It was published three weeks later, on January 31, simultaneously with Vanbrugh's fragment.[1]

The first edition (01), an octavo published by John Watts, gives the full text of the play as it was performed on the opening night; indeed, Cibber's prefatory epistle, dated January 27, draws attention to the fact that the reader will "find here a scene or two of the lower humor that were left out after the first day's presentation." For the first audience had been more than usually hostile to Cibber, and more than usually rowdy and censorious. Particular objection was taken to the scenes of "lower humor," which were mistakenly attributed to Cibber's sole authorship—an understandable error when Cibber himself was playing Sir Francis Wronghead, the country gentleman who travels to London to

---

[1] An advertisement printed beneath the cast-list in *The Provoked Husband* announces: "Jan. 31, 1727/8. *This Day is Publish'd, for the Satisfaction of the Curious,* A JOURNEY to *LONDON.* Being Part of a Comedy written by the Late Sir *John Vanbrugh*, Knt. and Printed after his own Copy . . . ." Cibber arranged for simultaneous publication so that the curious reader could assess his contribution to the play; as will appear below, he had not scrupled to mislead the curious spectator.

establish his own and his family's fortune. Cibber realized that cuts would have to be made immediately if the play was to succeed. Moreover, he took the unusual course of publishing the abridged text; shortly after the appearance of 01 he prepared what is in effect an unacknowledged second edition (02), also published in octavo by Watts. This evidently represents the play that was seen by audiences on the second and subsequent nights. In Act I Cibber removed three short passages of dialogue centering on the comic "low" character John Moody. Vanbrugh's emphasis on the word "soberly" in the conversation between Lady Townly and Lady Grace (Act III) was slightly reduced, so that Lady Grace should not sound absurdly insistent in her advocacy of a moderate way of life. The major omission, and the most surprising to a modern reader, was made in Act IV, where the delightful assignation and mock-betrothal scene between the bumpkin Squire Richard and the chambermaid Myrtilla was sacrificed to the wrath of the audience.

Neither Cibber nor his publisher chose to draw attention to the abridged edition, and it received no mention in the columns of contemporary newspapers and catalogues. As a result, the existence of these two distinct editions of 1728 has not always been recognized in modern bibliographies, nor has their relationship been investigated. It would seem that the printer of 02 worked from a copy of the first edition in which Cibber had marked the passages to be deleted. The text was not reset; alterations were made in the standing type, which was ingeniously and economically rearranged to fill the gaps and to preserve intact as many complete lines of type, and even entire pages, as possible. Since the same setting of type was being used, the title pages, preliminary matter, and the play-text as far as the end of page fourteen are identical in 01 and 02. For most of Act IV and the whole of Act V only repagination and new signatures were called for, though the opportunity was taken to make some small corrections. The most immediately apparent difference between the editions is that whereas in 01 the play occupies ninety-nine numbered pages, in 02 it takes up only ninety-five.

When he excised the "scene or two of the lower humor," however, Cibber forgot to remove the reference to them in his prefatory remarks. 02 therefore begins by announcing that it has restored the very passages which it in fact omits. It seems reasonable to regard this as a mere oversight on Cibber's part, concentrating as he was on alterations to the actual text of the play. For there is ample bibliographical evidence that 02 is the later edition, and not merely the product of a muddle in the printing-house whereby a shortened text was printed from the theater copy and later superseded by the full, authorized version. Some items of this evidence may be cited here. Most important, minor corrections were made during the preparation and printing of 02. The misprints "comsum'd" (01, p. 84) and "too" (for "to," p. 98) were put right before production of 02 began; "belive'd" (p. 87) was noticed during printing and appears correctly as "believ'd" in some copies of 02 (e.g., Bodleian M adds.108.e.100(5), and Worcester College AA.5.3); a word that had been omitted in 01 was supplied (see textual note on V.iv.132) and the type rearranged to accommodate it. Several small details of spacing and lay-out also clearly point to the priority of 01. Finally, certain distinctive features of 02, such as missing signatures and (in some copies) an inverted ornament between Acts II and III, could have resulted from accidents to the standing type while it was being corrected and rearranged.

Two changes which Cibber might have made for 02 are almost as remarkable as those which he did make. First: just after the assignation scene Mrs. Motherly offers to prepare a snack for Sir Francis: "Will you give me leave to get you a broiled bone, or so, till the ladies come home, sir?" On the opening night this bone so amused and scandalized the spectators that it brought the performance to a standstill.[2] Yet it survived in 02. Cibber's impenitence may be ascribed to the fact that responsibility for the offending bone lay with Vanbrugh, who, even more daringly, had given the phrase to Sir Francis's wife. The separate publication of *A Journey to London* thus exculpated Cibber; it also revealed that the assignation scene, all but one sentence, was entirely his own work, which explains why he considered it a fitter sop for Cerberus. Secondly, 02 retained all the curious infelicities of the prefatory address "To the Reader": Cibber was still proudly informing a "succession of our successors of the stage" that the

[2] See Benjamin Victor, *The History of the Theatres of London and Dublin* (London, 1761), II, 105; and Charles B. Woods, "Cibber in Fielding's *Author's Farce:* Three Notes," *Philological Quarterly,* XLIV (1965), 149–151.

actress Mrs. Oldfield *"here outdid* her usual *out-doing"* and wore on stage all the "paraphonalia" of a woman of quality. Yet Cibber's critics pounced on these lapses within weeks of the play's publication. As early as February 24, 1728, his inveterate enemy *Mist's Journal* ridiculed his bizarre prose, and in *The Art of Sinking in Poetry* (published on March 8) Pope carefully parodied the eulogy of Mrs. Oldfield by way of introducing a satirical attack on the contemporary theater.[3] As Cibber was not insensitive to such criticism we may infer that 02 followed so very hard on the heels of 01 that the hostile reactions had not yet appeared in print. Certainly by the time he came to prepare the "second edition" he was ready to mend his faults.

This "second edition" (03), so designated on its title page, was published on January 28, 1729, also by Watts, and from an entirely new setting of type.[4] It is a handsome and carefully printed octavo, with a frontispiece depicting the reconciliation scene (V.ii), engraved by Gerard Vandergucht. 03 contains one important addition to the text, Jenny's second song, in Act V. This, like her song in Act IV, was written by Henry Carey, and was heard for the first time on April 11, 1728, when the play-bills announced that the performance would include "The Romp's Song as usual, and a new Ballad, called The Fine Lady's Life." But 03 also reveals some interesting changes of heart. On the one hand the omitted sections of Act I and the assignation scene are restored; on the other, new concessions to contemporary taste are made. Myrtilla's bitter regrets about her seduction by Count Basset are toned down, and the broiled bone, which not even Vanbrugh's reputation could save, was neutralized to "a little something." The prose of the Preface became rather more orthodox in deference to the critics, stylistic improvements were made in the text, and a few grammatical slips and misprints were put right.

[3] The preface soon became a standing joke. It was of particular service to Cibber's foes when he was appointed Poet Laureate in 1730. See note to l. 110 of "To the Reader"; also *An Apology for the Life of Colley Cibber . . . Written by Himself,* ed. B. R. S. Fone (Ann Arbor, 1968), pp. 33–34; and Richard Hindry Barker, *Mr. Cibber of Drury Lane* (New York, 1939), pp. 157–159.

[4] Date of publication from *A Register of Books, 1728–1732, extracted from "The Monthly Chronicle,"* English Bibliographical Sources, series I, No. 3 (London, 1964), p. 26.

Cibber did not revise the play again. The numerous editions published in London during his lifetime follow the text of 03, and introduce only such variants as may be attributed to the hand of a compositor. These changes are of a kind familiar enough in the transmission of dramatic texts—"and" becomes "but," " 'twas" turns into "was"—and they follow a familiar pattern: since a new edition is usually based upon its immediate predecessor the corruptions are cumulative. In short, there is nothing in these editions to suggest the presence of a revising author. But if they are without textual significance they are at least pointers to the play's continuing popularity with readers as well as theater audiences. Between 1729 and 1757, the year of Cibber's death, six separate London editions had been called for. The comedy was also included in the collected edition of Vanbrugh's plays published in 1730. Two Dublin editions were published during 1728, and at about the same time the enterprising Thomas Johnson brought out a pirated text as part of his series of English plays published in Holland.

The "basic copy" for this edition is 01, specifically the copy in Edinburgh University Library; it has been collated with copies of 02 and 03.[5] I have incorporated readings from 03 wherever that text offers a stylistic improvement (as in the Preface) or an addition (the song in Act V). But in cases where Cibber seems merely to have succumbed to the squeamish taste of his audience (as in Myrtilla's soliloquy and the broiled bone), I have preferred to follow the more forthright and Vanbrugian first edition. Variants in later texts have been ignored, with the exceptions of a minor correction in the 1730 edition of Vanbrugh's plays, and a small grammatical emendation introduced into the separate

---

[5] I have collated copies in the British Museum Library (01–3), Bodleian Library (01, 02 [two copies], 03), Worcester College, Oxford (02, two copies), University of Cambridge Library (02), and Sion College, London (01). I have also examined copies of the following London editions (all duodecimos): 1734, 1735, 1740, 1741, 1748, and 1753, together with Vanbrugh's *Plays* (1730). I should add that the Yale University Library copy, reproduced in the Readex microprint *Three Centuries of Drama* series, is of 02; and that the text printed in Vol. III of *The Complete Works of Sir John Vanbrugh*, ed. Bonamy Dobrée and Geoffrey Webb (London, 1927–1928), is based upon 02 and 03 only.

edition of the play in 1735. I have adopted these corrections (at I.202, and II.111), but have not recorded other variants in the 1730 and 1735 texts.

The male Wrongheads and John Moody speak with more or less broad Yorkshire accents. Neither Vanbrugh nor Cibber attempted absolute consistency of spelling when representing dialect speech. Moody says "measter" and "mester," but also "master"; Squire Richard has "you" and "yow," "mother" and "moather." I have not attempted to impose regularity. I have, however, thought it necessary to lighten the remarkably heavy punctuation of the first edition. Sometimes, as in Squire Richard's laborious and halting speeches, Cibber is aiming at a comic effect, and I have retained as much as possible of this "characteristical" punctuation. Elsewhere, the pointing is intended to provide very precise guidance to the actors: dashes are liberally used to indicate significant pauses, and to leave room for stage business; emphasis is conveyed by italics, but more commonly by initial capitalizing of adjectives and verbs; a multitude of commas helps the actor by marking off key-words and phrases, and indicating the rhythms of the prose. So the pleasure-loving Lady Townly reproachfully asks her husband: "What can I, possibly, do, at home?" Cibber requires that the voice should linger, with a tone of incredulity, over the "I" and the "possibly," should utter the "do" with contemptuous disbelief, and come down with crushing emphasis on "at home." Such heavy punctuation tends to get in the way of the silent reader; I have tried to reduce it without departing too far from the spirit of Cibber's pointing. Finally, since the long fifth act falls naturally into four self-contained scenes, I have subdivided it accordingly.

Cibber's Prologue implies that *A Journey to London* was the product of Vanbrugh's mature years, a moral atonement for past licentiousness. But the Prologue, as we shall see, is not altogether trustworthy, and its tendentious suggestions, like those of the Preface, cannot be relied upon as evidence for the dating of Vanbrugh's fragment. The text of the fragment—assuming that Cibber published a faithful transcript of Vanbrugh's papers—yields some small clues: an allusion to the Septennial Act points to a date sometime after 1716, while references to the game of quadrille and to "toupees" suggest the early 1720s. It is therefore tempting to connect the play with Vanbrugh's letter to Jacob Tonson of June 18, 1722: the actors, he writes, are "forc'd to Act round and round upon the Old Stock, though Cibber tells me, 'tis not to be conceiv'd, how many and how bad Plays, are brought to them."[6] Perhaps it was in this mood of dissatisfaction with the sorry state of the London theater that *A Journey to London* was conceived;[7] or perhaps Cibber flatteringly encouraged Vanbrugh to take up again a project he had begun some years before.

All this is largely conjecture. What is certain is that the unfinished *Journey to London* is a short sketch of three and a half acts, rather less than half the length of *The Relapse*. Yet of the completed play only about a third derives from Vanbrugh, for Cibber did not simply expand and amplify; he dropped some lively, farcical material (the misadventures in the coach when the ladies go to the theater, and the hazard-playing scene) as well as whole passages of dialogue and several incidental touches of satire. These omissions allowed Cibber to develop and give prominence to the scenes between Lord and Lady Townly (Vanbrugh's Lord and Lady Loverule). It was in their quarrels and final reconciliation that his chief interest lay, whereas Vanbrugh's imagination had been stimulated by the arrival of his rustic fools in the metropolis of knaves. His provincial family, the Head-pieces, occupies the center of the stage: Cibber's Wrongheads are relegated to a subordinate position (and to the subtitle of the new play), though in reorganizing the action Cibber was careful to make one of his principal characters, Manly, intimately concerned in the fortunes of both the Wrongheads and the Townlys. There is some truth in Cibber's complaint that Vanbrugh's scenes were "undigested" or "irregular," a succession of brief, vigorous, but not always very clearly interrelated episodes. Cibber has given shape and form to the play by working up three major quarrels between the Townlys, each more intense and threatening than the last, interwoven with Manly's courtship of Lady Grace—two compatible temperaments whose domestic future seems bright—and the schemings of Lady Wronghead and Count Basset. Cibber has thus imposed regularity and symmetry, and has tied up the

[6] *Complete Works*, ed. Dobrée and Webb, IV, 146.
[7] Laurence Whistler, *Sir John Vanbrugh, Architect and Dramatist* (London, 1938), p. 291.

dramatic threads. He has also skilfully exploited the resources of the theater and the abilities of the Drury Lane company. His actors, himself included, are given opportunities for virtuoso display, as in the long speeches of Lord and Lady Townly and Sir Francis. And he has created a distinct theatrical tone for each act. The bustle of Act II contrasts with the duologues of Act III, while Act IV (like the fourth act of his *Careless Husband*) is full of conspiratorial whisperings and asides, with characters grouping and regrouping as the intrigue gathers momentum. The fifth act is distinguished by its use of scene-changes and spectacle; it affords a masquerade and a dance, as well as all the distress and suspense of the dènouement.

The contrast with Vanbrugh's *Journey to London* is very marked. His rapid scenes are full of activity, and of energy threatening to erupt. The fragment breaks off at the moment when Sir Francis interrupts the rakes and ladies in their hazard-playing; violence is imminent. In a sense it is only fitting that Vanbrugh's last play should be tantalizingly unfinished. It was the unreal sense of finality in Cibber's *Love's Last Shift*, the cheerful, even smug suggestion that nothing remains to be said, which irritated and amused him, and which prompted its "sequel," *The Relapse*. Now Cibber has the last word, substituting order and tidiness for Vanbrugh's explosiveness, imposing on the plot those dramatic qualities that Vanbrugh scorned. In 1698 Vanbrugh had entered an emphatic protest against "the too exact observance of what's call'd the Rules of the Stage, and the crowding a Comedy with a great deal of Intricate Plot." In his opinion, "the chief entertainment, as well as the Moral, lies much more in the Characters and the Dialogue, than in the Business and the Event."[8] Cibber is very much concerned with the plot and the moral lesson to be drawn from its resolution. Vanbrugh is preoccupied with the interaction of characters, especially in situations of potential or actual friction and hostility.

Throughout, Cibber has softened the rigors of the original. Vanbrugh is at pains to emphasize the nastier and harsher sides of London life, at the level both of the street and of the drawing room. The goose-pie, which has traveled with the Headpieces from

[8] *A Short Vindication of the Relapse and the Provok'd Wife, from Immorality and Prophaneness*, in *Complete Works*, ed. Dobrée and Webb, I, 209.

Yorkshire, is violently seized by two hungry rogues who are not afraid to set on their rustic pursuers. The rakish Captain Toupee, whom Cibber dispenses with entirely, indulges in rude familiarity with Lady Loverule. And Vanbrugh's Mrs. Motherly is "an errant Bawd," her lodgings no better than a brothel—so that the Headpieces may find themselves unawares in the same embarrassment that John Moody experienced on his earlier visit to London, when it appears he was kidnapped into a house of ill repute. Cibber has not a word of John Moody's escapades; the author of *Love's Last Shift* would not have scrupled to joke about them, but times and audiences have changed. Of Mrs. Motherly's profession only the merest hint remains in the name itself (Mother being the common title for a bawd), and in the phrase with which she leaves Myrtilla and the Squire to their tête-à-tête: "I'll even turn you together." Time and again Cibber takes the edge off Vanbrugh's forcefulness. It is a small but significant detail that Lady Loverule responds to Clarinda's account of an unfashionably sober way of spending one's life by remarking: "Well, Clarinda, thou art a most contemptible Creature." Lady Townly's reaction is: "Well, my dear, thou art an astonishing creature."[9] This is not to say that Lady Townly lacks spirit, but that she is spirited in a more polite and amiable way. She has a teasing, playful tone in many of her altercations with her husband, and takes an amused delight in seeing herself come off best. She is still the same coquette as in her youth; for just as a coquette values her chastity only for the bargaining power it gives her, so Lady Townly is conscious that she can make capital out of her fidelity to her husband.[10] Lady Loverule is altogether tougher, more aggressive, more caustic of tongue. The depths of her nature are uncovered in a brief, harsh scene which Cibber omits, an interview with her mercer in which the sardonic lady merrily taunts the poor fellow into a passion. It is, however, typical of Vanbrugh's complex attitude that the mercer, Mr. Shortyard, is not simply an innocent victim of upper-class callousness; his very

[9] This example is also quoted by Barker in his valuable account of Cibber's modifications of the main characters: see *Mr. Cibber of Drury Lane*, pp. 142–145.

[10] The point is emphasized by a deliberate and unusual verbal echo: at III. 354–356 Lord Townly admonishes his wife with the same argument that Manly has used a little earlier in conversation with Lady Grace (ll. 138–140).

name passes judgment on him (unlike Cibber's neutral "Mr. Lutestring"). Again, Vanbrugh's principal villain, Colonel Courtly, has about him some of the cynicism and audacity of his Restoration forebears, whereas Count Basset, for all his sprightly metaphors from the card-table, is merely the smooth insinuating sharper. He cringes in defeat as the Colonel would never have done.

In the Prologue Cibber alleges that Vanbrugh, as he grew older, rejected his earlier views about morality and comedy. A play, he came to believe, should explicitly punish vice, and hold up to the spectators images not only of what they are but also of what they ought to be. This certainly runs quite counter to Vanbrugh's sturdy self-defense in the *Short Vindication*: "The Business of Comedy is to shew People what they shou'd do, by representing them upon the Stage, doing what they shou'd not."[11] That doctrine is in fact restated by one of the characters in *A Journey to London*—"Bad Examples (if they are but bad enough) give us as useful Reflections as good ones do"—and there is no evidence in the play itself, or in what Cibber discloses of Vanbrugh's intentions, to suggest a change of heart. Cibber is falsely ascribing to Vanbrugh his own faith in exemplary comedy, a faith for which he was to be tellingly rebuked by Fielding in connection with this very play.[12] The Prologue is quite misleading, suggesting a nonexistent affinity between the two dramatists. For from what Cibber says in his introductory remarks it is clear that the *Journey to London* was heading in a different direction from that taken by *The Provoked Husband*. Vanbrugh apparently planned to bring the Loverule quarrel to a climax (and in all probability to allow Lady Loverule to "make the House ring with Reprisals," as her husband predicts), before having him actually "turn her out of his doors." Their antagonism was to issue in an angry separation, without hope of reconciliation, but also without the possibility of divorce, since although the lady lives dangerously among familiar coxcombs and sharpers, she has not been unfaithful. Had Vanbrugh finished the play the high-life plot would have been a bleak study of marital incompatibility and disillusionment, a case of what Cibber calls "adultery of the

[11] Edn. cit., p. 206.
[12] *Tom Jones*, Book XII, ch. 5; the most searching and skilful of Fielding's many attacks on Cibber.

mind." And no doubt the successful Sir Charles/Clarinda relationship would have stood over against the misery of the Loverules much as the two pairs in *The Provoked Wife* are contrasted with one another. In Cibber's hands the play has become a triumph of conventional morality, and of the marriage vow. Lady Townly at last begins to love her husband; more important, she learns to honor and obey him. The difference between the two endings was nicely put by the anonymous author of the first serious critique of the play, *Reflections on the Principal Characters in . . . "The Provoked Husband"*: Vanbrugh's solution to the dilemma "would have answer'd to our judgments, the other sooth[e]s our good Nature."[13]

Cibber was quite explicit about his reasons for so drastically altering the projected course of the plot. He thought that "such violent measures" as Lord Loverule would have taken, "however just they might be in real life, were too severe for comedy, and would want the proper surprise which is due to the end of a play." Surprise of this kind was not a quality that much interested Vanbrugh, who found material rather in the impulses and obstinacies of "real life." Cibber prefers the less painful way of an eleventh-hour reformation, though in order to excite our emotions he brings us to the brink of catastrophe. The anonymous essayist observed that Cibber had "carried the severe part so far, as with the Help of the Action [i.e., acting] to draw Tears from the Eyes of his Audience, which surely can never be the natural Business of Comedy"; he might therefore "have safely ventured one Step farther."[14] But Cibber had by now a whole series of reconciliation scenes behind him—in *Love's Last Shift, The Careless Husband, The Lady's Last Stake*; the formula was well-tried and successful. He clearly enjoyed working up these scenes, with their emotionalism and religiose language. "Save me, hide me from the world!" exclaims Lady Townly; and again: "How odious does this goodness make me!" Her reformation is scarcely pre-

[13] *Reflections* (London, 1728), p. 11. The "other" solution is found also in Charles Johnson's *The Masquerade* (1719); the author of the *Reflections* plausibly argues Cibber's indebtedness to that play, which in turn owes something to Shirley's *Lady of Pleasure* (1637). The *Reflections*, a thirty-two page pamphlet, was published on April 6, 1728; the only copy I have traced is in the Widener Library of Harvard University.

[14] *Reflections*, p. 21.

pared for (the twinges of remorse and regret she experiences in Act III are too slight to be of much consequence), and is to that extent a sentimental simplification.[15] But in fairness to Cibber it must be said that he is not inviting the audience to wallow in the merely distressful; tears are shed over a sinner's moral reformation, not over undeserved misfortune.

Meanwhile the "scenes of the lower humor" are running their largely separate course, demanding a very different set of responses from the audience. It is true that some parallels are established between the spendthrift wives and their overindulgent, and finally provoked, husbands: Lady Wronghead's preference for wax candles is neatly matched by Lady Townly's extravagant demand for white flambeaux, and neither lady chooses to have a head for figures. But whereas Lady Townly can be brought, after some emotional bullying, to a sorrowful sense of her follies, Lady Wronghead can only be blackmailed into a temporary docility. So the Wronghead family is left in a state of uneasy truce, having learnt only the first half of the play's moral lesson: "Let husbands govern, gentle wives obey." Nor is there much hope that Lady Wronghead will come to appreciate the charm of that domestic "sobriety" which Lady Grace champions in her dialogue with Lady Townly (Act III), and which runs as a subdued theme throughout the play. The Epilogue too reminds us of the merit of Lady Grace's "comfortable scheme of life": six months of sober living in the country, followed by a sober six months in London. It is characteristic of Cibber that the play should end on a note of moderate compromise, and perhaps this is one reason for its success during the eighteenth century. The manners and persons of the main plot are ostensibly upper class, yet the sobriety which is advocated is essentially a middle-class virtue, the virtue of the citizen and the merchant who frown on extravagance. Like Richardson, Cibber has a horror of the frivolities and irresponsibilities of high life (especially when they are concentrated in the treacherous inanities of the masquerade), even while he admires the glamor of polite society. As in *Pamela* we can enjoy the best of both social worlds; we can contentedly endorse the middle-class

[15] The scene illustrates many of the points made by Paul E. Parnell in "The Sentimental Mask," *PMLA*, LXXVIII (1963), 529–535; reprinted in *Restoration Drama: Modern Essays in Criticism*, ed. John Loftis (New York, 1966), pp. 285–297.

values which the plot upholds, while at the same time we breathe the more rarefied air in which the other, genteeler half lives.

The play has something for many, if not all, tastes: plot intrigue and strongly contrasted characters; wit without bawdy and virtuous sentiment without excessive mawkishness. And it has enough "low" humor for us to suppose that Goldsmith had it particularly in mind when he commended that kind of "Laughing and even Low Comedy, which seems to have been last exhibited by Vanbrugh and Cibber."[16] Hugh Blair went even further; he thought *The Provoked Husband* "perhaps, on the whole, the best Comedy in the English Language."[17]

On the opening night, only the Townly plot, erroneously thought to be Vanbrugh's main contribution, was well received. Vexatious as the noisy interruptions must have been, Cibber had the gratification of seeing the reconciliation scene win the audience's sympathy, and of hearing the conclusion "greatly and generously applauded."[18] His enemies were quick to remark that the work owed all its success to the actors. It certainly owed much to them; like all Cibber's plays it was written by an actor for actors, specifically for actors whose talents he was familiar with. Wilks, who created the part of Lord Townly, "was so much the real fine gentleman, that, in the scene where he was reduced to the necessity of reproaching Lady Townly with her faults, in his warmest anger he mixed such tenderness as was softened into tears"; and Mrs. Oldfield's Lady Townly was universally acknowledged "to be her *ne plus ultra* in acting."[19] Her part in the play's success was recognized by a handsome gift of fifty guineas from the Drury Lane management.[20]

The comedy had to make its way against opposition both inside the playhouse and out. The rival company at Lincoln's Inn Fields presented a short season of genuine Vanbrugh to expose

[16] "An Essay on the Theatre," *Collected Works of Oliver Goldsmith*, ed. Arthur Friedman (Oxford, 1966), III, 210.

[17] *Lectures on Rhetoric and Belles Lettres* (London, 1783), II, 545. The play was translated into German in 1753 and into French in 1761: DeWitt C. Croissant, *Studies in the Works of Colley Cibber*, Humanistic Studies of the University of Kansas, vol. I (Lawrence, Kansas, 1915), p. 26.

[18] Thomas Davies, *Dramatic Miscellanies* (London, 1785 edn.), III, 466.

[19] Ibid., pp. 468 and 467.

[20] Cibber's *Apology*, ed. Fone, p. 168.

the hybrid at Drury Lane, and with malicious wit selected *The Confederacy* to coincide with the first night of *The Provoked Husband*. Such efforts were of little avail. Nine days after it opened Mrs. Delany was writing enthusiastically about "the new play, which is very much applauded, every body that has seen it commends it extremely."[21] The royal family attended the performance on January 27. At the end of the record opening run of twenty-eight performances the play had brought in over £140.[22]

Inevitably it was chosen to open the two following seasons at Drury Lane, where it remained an important part of the repertoire.[23] In the 1746–1747 season, for example, it received twenty-one performances in London, of which sixteen were at Drury Lane. It was successful at Dublin, and in 1765 was chosen for the first production at the new Theatre Royal, York. Naturally so popular a play attracted many of the most talented actors and actresses of the period. Quin appeared as Manly, and Garrick as a rather restrained Lord Townly. Penkethman and Macklin played Sir Francis, the latter to great effect: "Where he affected to be very wise, a laborious, emphatic slyness marked the endeavour humorously."[24] Peg Woffington, and later Elizabeth Farren, came near to rivaling Mrs. Oldfield's Lady Townly. Although Mrs. Siddons never took part in a London production of the play, she gave a solo reading of its most famous scenes for the royal family: "She introduced John Moody's account of the journey and read it admirably. The part of Lord and Lady Townly's reconciliation, she worked up finely, and made it very affecting."[25]

The play that was so successful was not, however, always quite

---

[21] *The Autobiography and Correspondence of Mary Granville, Mrs. Delany*, ed. Lady Llanover (London, 1861), I, 153.

[22] *Apology*, ed. Fone, p. 284.

[23] The following brief account of the play's stage history owes a great deal to *The London Stage, 1660–1800*, Part II, ed. Emmett L. Avery, and Part III, ed. Arthur H. Scouten (Carbondale, Ill., 1960 and 1961), and to the section "Theatrical History" in *Complete Works of Vanbrugh*, ed. Dobrée and Webb, III, 172–176.

[24] Francis Gentleman, *The Dramatic Censor* (London, 1770), I, 210–211.

[25] *Autobiography of Mrs. Delany*, second series (London, 1862), III, 254–255; the reading was given on May 9, 1785.

the same play that it had been in 1728. Most performances would seem to have followed Cibber's lead in omitting what were considered the grosser speeches of John Moody. To judge from acting editions, like that of 1765, and texts where "cuts in performance" are marked, it was common practice towards the end of the eighteenth century to omit some or all of the following: (1) Moody's description in Act I of the education of the young Wrongheads; (2) the smoking and drinking episode at the end of Act II; (3) the dialogue in Act III on coquettes and prudes; (4) both songs; (5) the opening dialogue of V.i; and (6) the masquerade scene. If the masquerade was retained it was usually placed before the reconciliation of the Townlys, so that that heartwarming scene could bring the comedy to a fitting close. According to the edition of 1808 this alteration "much improves the general effect."[26]

At the beginning of the nineteenth century the play was still very much alive. Charles Kemble and Macready triumphantly played Lord Townly to the Lady Townly of Ellen Tree and Helen Faucit. But soon thereafter its popularity began to wane. Though it kept the stage in the provinces until the later part of the century, it was last performed in London during the 1858–1859 season, when Phelps appeared as Lord Townly at Sadler's Wells.[27] With that, the play that had been praised as the best English comedy passed from the professional London stage.

During the preparation of this edition friends and colleagues have most generously given me their expert help and advice; I am particularly indebted to John Barnard, Antony Coleman, David Mills, Matthew Port, and John Ross. I am also grateful to the University of London for a grant from its Central Research Fund, and to the many librarians in England and America who kindly answered my enquiries, and made microfilm and photocopies available to me.

PETER DIXON

Westfield College, London

[26] *The Provok'd Husband . . . Adapted for Theatrical Representation. With Selected and Original Anecdotes and Illustrations* (London, 1808), p. viii.

[27] Montague Summers, *A Bibliography of the Restoration Drama* (London, [1935]), p. 3; and *Complete Works of Vanbrugh*, ed. Dobrée and Webb, III, 176.

THE PROVOKED HUSBAND

Vivit tanquam vicina mariti.

Juv. Sat. VI.

Vivit . . . mariti] The woman who is extravagant and thriftless *lives as if she were her husband's neighbor* and not his wife. Juvenal, *Satire* VI, 509.

To the Queen

May it please Your Majesty,

The English theater throws itself, with this play, at Your Majesty's feet, for favor and support.

As their public diversions are a strong indication of   5
the genius of a people, the following scenes are an attempt to establish such as are fit to entertain the minds of a sensible nation, and to wipe off that aspersion of barbarity which the *virtuosi* among our neighbors have sometimes thrown upon our taste.   10

The Provoked Husband is at least an instance that an English comedy may, to an unusual number of days, bring many thousands of His Majesty's good subjects together, to their emolument and delight, with innocence. And however little share of that merit my unequal   15
pen may pretend to, yet I hope the just admirers of Sir John Vanbrugh will allow I have, at worst, been a careful guardian of his orphan muse, by leading it into Your Majesty's royal protection.

The design of this play being chiefly to expose and   20
reform the licentious irregularities that too often break in upon the peace and happiness of the married state, where could so hazardous and unpopular an undertaking be secure, but in the protection of a Princess whose exemplary conjugal virtues have given such illustrious proof   25
of what sublime felicity that holy state is capable?

And though a crown is no certain title to content, yet to the honor of that institution be it said, the royal harmony of hearts that now enchants us from the throne

---

1. *the Queen*] Caroline, wife of George II. She was interested in literature, and encouraged writers with her patronage.

8. *sensible*] judicious and sensitive.

9. *virtuosi*] connoisseurs, especially the trifling and finical kind.

12. *unusual . . . days*] The play had an initial run of twenty-eight performances, a record that was almost immediately broken by *The Beggar's Opera*.

14. *emolument*] advantage, profit.

15. *unequal*] inferior, inadequate.

is a reproach to the frequent disquiet of those many 30
insensible subjects about it, who (from His Majesty's
paternal care of his people) have more leisure to be
happy; and 'tis our Queen's peculiar glory that we
often see her as eminently raised above her circle in
private happiness as in dignity.   35

Yet heaven, Madam, that has placed you on such
height to be the more conspicuous pattern of your sex,
had still left your happiness imperfect, had it not given
those inestimable treasures of your mind and person to
the only Prince on earth that could have deserved them. 40
A crown received from any but the happy monarch's
hand who invested you with this, which you now adorn,
had only seemed the work of Fortune; but *thus* be-
stowed, the world acknowledges it the due reward of
Providence for one you once so gloriously refused.   45

But as the fame of such elevated virtue has lifted the
plain addresses of a whole nation into eloquence, the
best repeated eulogiums on that theme are but intru-
sions on Your Majesty's greater pleasure of secretly deserving them. I therefore beg leave to subscribe myself, 50
           May it please Your Majesty,
                Your Majesty's most devoted,
                   Most obedient, and
                      Most humble servant,
                               COLLEY CIBBER   55

---

34. *circle*] the privileged inner group of courtiers and ladies who
surrounded the Queen at her levees and at receptions in the royal
drawing room.

45. *one . . . refused*] Caroline had withdrawn from an arranged marriage with Charles of Spain (afterwards Emperor Charles VI) which
would have meant changing her religion.

47. *addresses*] the loyal addresses presented by public figures, civic
corporations, etc., to George II and his queen on their accession to
the throne in June, 1727.

To the Reader

Having taken upon me, in the prologue to this play, to give the auditors some short account of that part of it which Sir John Vanbrugh left unfinished, and not thinking it advisable in that place to limit their judg- 5
ment by so high a commendation as I thought it deserved, I have therefore, for the satisfaction of the curious, printed the whole of what he wrote, separately, under the single title he gave it, of *A Journey to London*, without presuming to alter a line; which the 10
bookseller will sell with, or without, *The Provoked Husband*.

Yet when I own that in my last conversation with him (which chiefly turned upon what he had done towards a comedy) he excused his not showing it me 15
till he had reviewed it, confessing the scenes were yet undigested, too long and irregular, particularly in the lower characters, I have but one excuse for publishing what he never designed should come into the world, as it then was—viz., I had no other way of taking those 20
many faults to myself which may be justly found in my presuming to finish it.

However, a judicious reader will find, in his original papers, that the characters are strongly drawn, new, spirited, and natural, taken from sensible observations 25
on high and lower life, and from a just indignation at the follies in fashion. All I could gather from him of what he intended in the catastrophe, was that the conduct of his imaginary fine lady had so provoked him that he designed actually to have made her husband turn 30
her out of his doors. But when his performance came (after his decease) to my hands, I thought such violent measures, however just they might be in real life, were too severe for comedy, and would want the proper surprise which is due to the end of a play. Therefore with 35

10–12. which . . . *Husband*] om. in   26. at] *03*; of *01–2*.
all edns. after 03.

5. *limit*] influence, predetermine.

much ado (and 'twas as much as I could do, with probability) I preserved the lady's chastity, that the sense of
her errors might make a reconciliation not impracticable;
and I hope the mitigation of her sentence has been,
since, justified by its success.   40

My inclination to preserve as much as possible of
Sir John, I soon saw had drawn the whole into an
unusual length; the reader will therefore find here a
scene or two of the lower humor that were left out after
the first day's presentation.   45

The favor the town has shown to the higher characters in this play is a proof that their taste is not
wholly vitiated by the barbarous entertainments that
have been so expensively set off to corrupt it. But while
the repetition of the best old plays is apt to give satiety, 50
and good new ones are so scarce a commodity, we must
not wonder that the poor actors are sometimes forced to
trade in trash for a livelihood.

I cannot yet take leave of the reader without endeavor-
ing to do justice to those principal actors who have so   55
evidently contributed to the support of this comedy. And
I wish I could separate the praises due to them, from
the secret vanity of an author; for all I can say will still
insinuate that they could not have so highly excelled,
unless the skill of the writer had given them proper   60
occasion. However, as I had rather appear vain than
unthankful, I will venture to say of Mr. Wilks that, in
the last act, I never saw any passion take so natural a
possession of an actor, or any actor take so tender a

43–45. *a scene . . . presentation*] See Introduction, pp. xiii–xiv.

48. *entertainments*] pantomimes (though the term also covered
farces and other theatrical afterpieces). Cibber is being disingenuous:
the pantomimes of the rival company at Lincoln's Inn Fields were
more spectacular and better patronized, but Drury Lane produced its
share of these very profitable barbarisms.

49. *set off*] presented on the stage.

62. *Mr. Wilks*] Robert Wilks (ca. 1665–1732), leading actor and joint
manager of the Drury Lane company. He excelled in portraying fine
gentlemen, and was renowned for his graceful exits. Elsewhere Cibber
praised his skill in scenes of pathos and tenderness (*Apology*, pp. 314–
315).

possession of his auditors. Mr. Mills, too, is confessed by   65
everybody to have surprised them, by so far excelling
himself. But there is no doing right to Mrs. Oldfield,
without putting people in mind of what others, of great
merit, have wanted to come near her. 'Tis not enough
to say she *here outdid* her usual *excellence*. I might   70
therefore justly leave her to the constant admiration of
those spectators who have the pleasure of living while
she is an actress. But as this is not the only time she has
been the life of what I have given the public, so perhaps
my saying a little more of so memorable an actress may   75
give this play a chance to be read, when the people of
this age shall be ancestors. May it therefore give emula-
tion to our successors of the stage to know that, to
the ending of the year 1727, a cotemporary comedian
relates that Mrs. Oldfield was then in her highest excel-   80
lence of action, happy in all the rarely-found requisites
that meet in one person to complete them for the stage.
She was in stature just rising to that height where the
graceful can only begin to show itself; of a lively aspect,
and a command in her mien that, like the principal   85
figure in the finest paintings, first seizes and longest
delights the eye of the spectator. Her voice was sweet,

70. *excellence*] *03*; out-doing *01–2*.   78. to our successors] *03*; to a
                                            succession of our successors *01–2*.

65. *Mr. Mills*] John Mills (died 1736), a diligent but uninspired
actor, specializing in serious roles. He was a protégé of Wilks—which
may account for Cibber's guarded compliment.
67. *Mrs. Oldfield*] Anne Oldfield (1683–1730), a brilliant and versa-
tile actress, and a mainstay of the Drury Lane company.
73–74. *not the only . . . public*] In 1704 she had created the part of
Lady Betty Modish in Cibber's *Careless Husband*. Since then she had
played Lady Dainty in his *Double Gallant*, Mrs. Conquest in *The
Lady's Last Stake*, and Maria in *The Non-juror*.
79. *cotemporary*] Though Pope ridiculed Cibber for using this variant of *contemporary* (*The Art of Sinking in Poetry*, ch. xvi), the
form had in fact become "so prevalent after *c.* 1725, as almost to expel
contemporary from use" (*OED*). Its popularity waned rapidly after
1800.
79. *comedian*] an actor (not necessarily a comic one), or a writer
of comedies; Cibber was both.

strong, piercing, and melodious; her pronunciation voluble, distinct, and musical, and her emphasis always
placed where the spirit of the sense, in her periods, only   90
demanded it. If she delighted more in the higher comic
than the tragic strain, 'twas because the last is too often
written in a lofty disregard of nature. But in characters
of modern practiced life she found occasions to add the
particular air and manner which distinguished the differ-   95
ent humors she presented; whereas in tragedy the manner
of speaking varies as little as the blank verse it is
written in. She had one peculiar happiness from nature: she looked and maintained the *agreeable* at a time
when other fine women only raise admirers by their   100
understanding. The spectator was always as much
informed by her eyes as her elocution; for the look is
the only proof that an actor rightly conceives what he
utters, there being scarce an instance where the eyes do
their part, that the elocution is known to be faulty. The   105
qualities she had *acquired*, were the *genteel* and the
elegant. The one in her air, and the other in her dress,
never had her equal on the stage; and the ornaments she
herself provided (particularly in this play) seemed in
all respects the paraphernalia of a woman of quality.   110
And of that sort were the characters she chiefly excelled

110. paraphernalia] *03*; paraphonalia *01–2*.

88–89. *voluble*] smooth, fluent.
94. *practiced*] as it is practiced, as it really is.
96. *humors*] characters, dispositions.
102. *her eyes*] Mrs. Oldfield had large and expressive eyes, and a
way of half-closing them for comic effect (Thomas Davies, *Dramatic
Miscellanies* [London, 1785 ed.], III. 461–462).
110. *paraphernalia*] used here in its restricted (originally legal) sense
of a wife's personal property, clothes, jewels, etc. The form of the
word was far from settled in the seventeenth and eighteenth centuries,
and the spelling *paraphonalia* (see textual note) had been thought
perfectly proper during the Restoration period. Fielding, however,
considered it an irresistibly comic Cibberian blunder (see, for example,
The Author's Farce, ed. Charles B. Woods [Lincoln, Nebr., 1966],
III.670 ff.; and the Preface to *Tom Thumb*, ed. L. J. Morrissey [Edin-
burgh, 1970], p. 17).

in; but her natural good sense, and lively turn of conversation, made her way so easy to ladies of the highest
rank, that it is a less wonder if on the stage she sometimes *was*, what might have become the finest woman in 115
real life to have supported.

C. Cibber

Theatre Royal, Jan. 27, 1728

113–114. *made her way . . . rank*] gave her ready access, in private
life, to the company of aristocratic ladies.

PROLOGUE

Spoken by Mr. Wilks

This play took birth from principles of truth,
To make amends for errors past, of youth.
A bard, that's now no more, in riper days
Conscious reviewed the license of his plays;
And though applause his wanton muse had fired,   5
Himself condemned what sensual minds admired.
At length he owned, that plays should let you see
Not only what you are, but ought to be:
Though vice was natural, 'twas never meant
The stage should show it, but for punishment.   10
Warm with that thought, his Muse once more took flame,
Resolved to bring licentious life to shame.
Such was the piece his latest pen designed,
But left no traces of his plan behind.
Luxuriant scenes, unpruned, or half contrived,   15
Yet, through the mass, his native fire survived;
Rough, as rich ore in mines, the treasure lay,
Yet still 'twas rich, and forms at length a play;
In which the bold compiler boasts no merit,
But that his pains have saved you scenes of spirit,   20
Not scenes that would a noisy joy impart,
But such as hush the mind, and warm the heart.
From praise of hands no sure account he draws,
But fixed attention is sincere applause.
If then (for hard you'll own the task) his art   25
Can to those embryon scenes new life impart,
The living proudly would exclude his lays,
And to the buried bard resign the praise.

3–4. *A bard . . . plays*] i.e., the mature Vanbrugh was conscience-stricken and guilty (*conscious*) as he looked over the licentious plays he had written as a young man. Cibber probably has in mind Vanbrugh's revision (in 1725) of two scenes in *The Provoked Wife* (see *Apology*, pp. 308–309, and *Provoked Wife*, ed. Zimansky, Appendix B).

27. *exclude his lays*] set aside his own contribution to the play.

DRAMATIS PERSONAE

LORD TOWNLY, of a regular life   *Mr. Wilks*

LADY TOWNLY, immoderate in her pur-   *Mrs. Oldfield*
suit of pleasures

LADY GRACE, sister to Lord Townly, of   *Mrs. Porter*
exemplary virtue

MR. MANLY, her admirer   *Mr. Mills, Senior*

SIR FRANCIS WRONGHEAD, a country   *Mr. Cibber, Senior*
gentleman

LADY WRONGHEAD, his wife; inclined to   *Mrs. Thurmond*
be a fine lady

SQUIRE RICHARD, his son; a mere whelp   *Young Wetherelt*

MISS JENNY, his daughter; pert, and for-   *Mrs. Cibber*
ward

JOHN MOODY, his servant; an honest   *Mr. Miller*
clown

COUNT BASSET, a gamester   *Mr. Bridgwater*

MRS. MOTHERLY, one that lets lodgings   *Mrs. Moore*

MYRTILLA, her niece, seduced by the   *Mrs. Grace*
Count

MRS. TRUSTY, Lady Townly's woman   *Mrs. Mills*

MASQUERADERS, CONSTABLE, SERVANTS, ETC.

The Scene: *Lord Townly's house,*
and sometimes Sir Francis's lodgings

The Provoked Husband

or

A Journey to London

ACT I

Scene: Lord Townly's apartment.
Lord Townly *solus.*

LORD TOWNLY.

Why did I marry? Was it not evident my plain, rational
scheme of life was impracticable, with a woman of so
different a way of thinking? Is there one article of it
that she has not broke in upon? Yes, let me do her
justice—her reputation; *that* I have no reason to believe   5
is in question. But then, how long her profligate course
of pleasures may make her able to keep it—is a shocking
question! And her presumption while she keeps it—
insupportable! For on the pride of that single virtue she
seems to lay it down, as a fundamental point, that the   10
free indulgence of every other vice this fertile town
affords is the birthright prerogative of a woman of
quality. Amazing, that a creature so warm in the pursuit
of her pleasures should never cast one thought towards
her happiness. Thus, while she admits no lover, she   15
thinks it a greater merit still, in her chastity, not to care
for her husband; and while she herself is solacing in one
continual round of cards and good company, he, poor
wretch, is left at large to take care of his own content-
ment. 'Tis time, indeed, some care were taken, and   20
speedily there shall be. Yet let me not be rash. Perhaps

---

17. *solacing*] having a gay and enjoyable time.

this disappointment of my heart may make me too impatient; and some tempers, when reproached, grow more untractable. —Here she comes. Let me be calm awhile.

Enter Lady Townly.

LORD TOWNLY.

Going out so soon after dinner, madam?   25

LADY TOWNLY.

Lard, my lord, what can I possibly do, at home?

LORD TOWNLY.

What does my sister, Lady Grace, do at home?

LADY TOWNLY.

Why, that is to me amazing! Have you ever any pleasure at home?

LORD TOWNLY.

It might be in your power, madam, I confess, to make it   30
a little more comfortable to me.

LADY TOWNLY.

Comfortable! And so, my good lord, you would really have a woman of my rank and spirit stay at home to comfort her husband? Lord, what notions of life some men have!   35

LORD TOWNLY.

Don't you think, madam, some ladies' notions are full as extravagant?

LADY TOWNLY.

Yes my lord, when the tame doves live cooped within the pen of your precepts, I do think 'em prodigious indeed.

LORD TOWNLY.

And when they fly wild about this town, madam, pray   40
what must the world think of 'em then?

LADY TOWNLY.

Oh, this world is not so ill-bred as to quarrel with any woman for liking it.

LORD TOWNLY.

Nor am I, madam, a husband so well-bred as to bear my wife's being so fond of it. In short, the life you lead,   45
madam—

---

26. *Lard*] a fashionable pronunciation.

LADY TOWNLY.

Is, to me, the pleasantest life in the world.

LORD TOWNLY.

I should not dispute your taste, madam, if a woman had
a right to please nobody but herself.

LADY TOWNLY.

Why, whom would you have her please?   50

LORD TOWNLY.

Sometimes, her husband.

LADY TOWNLY.

And don't you think a husband under the same obligation?

LORD TOWNLY.

Certainly.

LADY TOWNLY.

Why then we are agreed, my lord. For if I never go   55
abroad till I am weary of being at home (which you
know is the case), is it not equally reasonable not to
come home till one's aweary of being abroad?

LORD TOWNLY.

If this be your rule of life, madam, 'tis time to ask you
one serious question.   60

LADY TOWNLY.

Don't let it be long a-coming then, for I am in haste.

LORD TOWNLY.

Madam, when I am serious, I expect a serious answer.

LADY TOWNLY.

Before I know the question?

LORD TOWNLY.

Pshah! Have I power, madam, to make you serious by
entreaty?   65

LADY TOWNLY.

You have.

LORD TOWNLY.

And you promise to answer me sincerely?

LADY TOWNLY.

Sincerely.

LORD TOWNLY.

Now then, recollect your thoughts, and tell me seriously,
why you married me.   70

LADY TOWNLY.

You insist upon truth, you say?

LORD TOWNLY.

I think I have a right to it.

LADY TOWNLY.

Why then, my lord, to give you at once a proof of my obedience and sincerity—I think—I married—to take off that restraint that lay upon my pleasures while I was a 75 single woman.

LORD TOWNLY.

How, madam! Is any woman under less restraint after marriage, than before it?

LADY TOWNLY.

Oh my lord, my lord, they are quite different creatures. Wives have infinite liberties in life, that would be 80 terrible in an unmarried woman to take.

LORD TOWNLY.

Name one.

LADY TOWNLY.

Fifty, if you please. To begin then, in the morning: a married woman may have men at her toilet, invite them to dinner, appoint them a party in a stage box at the 85 play, engross the conversation there, call 'em by their Christian names, talk louder than the players; from thence jaunt into the City, take a frolicsome supper at an India-house, perhaps (in her *gaieté de coeur*) toast a pretty fellow, then clatter again to this end of town, 90 break with the morning into an assembly, crowd to the

---

80. *infinite*] a vogue-word of the period.

85. *stage box*] There were two stage boxes, one at each side of the proscenium: their occupants could see, and be seen, to perfection.

88. *City*] the business center of London. It was commonly contrasted with the fashionable west *end of town* (l.90).

89. *India-house*] a shop specializing in Oriental wares—tea, porcelain, silks, etc. These shops had gained some notoriety as places for assignations and intrigues.

89. *gaieté de coeur*] high spirits, irresponsible merriment.

91. *assembly*] a private party, usually devoted to card-playing and gossip.

hazard table, throw a familiar levant upon some sharp
lurching man of quality, and if he demands his money,
turn it off with a loud laugh, and cry—you'll owe it him,
to vex him. Ha ha!   95

LORD TOWNLY (*aside*).

Prodigious!

LADY TOWNLY.

These now, my lord, are some few of the many modish
amusements that distinguish the privilege of a wife from
that of a single woman.

LORD TOWNLY.

Death! Madam, what law has made these liberties less 100
scandalous in a wife than an unmarried woman?

LADY TOWNLY.

Why the strongest law in the world: custom—custom
time out of mind, my lord.

LORD TOWNLY.

Custom, madam, is the law of fools; but it shall never
govern me.   105

LADY TOWNLY.

Nay then, my lord, it's time for me to observe the laws
of prudence.

LORD TOWNLY.

I wish I could see an instance of it.

LADY TOWNLY.

You shall have one this moment, my lord. For I think,
when a man begins to lose his temper at home, if a 110
woman has any prudence, why—she'll go abroad till he
comes to himself again.   *Going.*

LORD TOWNLY.

Hold, madam! I am amazed you are not more uneasy at
the life we lead. You don't want sense, and yet seem

101. a wife] *03*; any wife *01–2.*

---

92. *hazard*] a dice game in which any number of players can take
part. It was the most popular form of gaming at this time.

92. *familiar levant*] "To throw a levant" (gamblers' slang) is to make
a bet without any intention of paying if one loses. *Familiar* may simply
mean "common, usual," the sort of thing everyone does; or perhaps
"unceremonious," the sort of thing one might do to an acquaintance.

93. *lurching*] cheating (like Lord Lurcher, 1.122, below).

void of all humanity; for with a blush I say it, I think 115
I have not wanted love.

LADY TOWNLY.

Oh don't say that, my lord, if you suppose I have my
senses!

LORD TOWNLY.

What is it I have done to you? What can you complain
of?   120

LADY TOWNLY.

Oh, nothing in the least. 'Tis true, you have heard me
say I have owed my Lord Lurcher an hundred pound
these three weeks—but what then—a husband is not
liable to his wife's debts of honor, you know, and if a
silly woman will be uneasy about money she can't be sued 125
for, what's that to him? As long as he loves her, to be
sure, she can have nothing to complain of.

LORD TOWNLY.

By heaven, if my whole fortune, thrown into your lap,
could make you delight in the cheerful duties of a wife,
I should think myself a gainer by the purchase.   130

LADY TOWNLY.

That is, my lord, I might receive your whole estate,
provided you were sure I would not spend a shilling of
it.

LORD TOWNLY.

No, madam. Were I master of your heart, your pleasures
would be mine; but different as they are, I'll feed even 135
your follies to deserve it. Perhaps you may have some
other trifling debts of honor abroad, that keep you out
of humor at home. At least it shall not be my fault if I
have not more of your company—there, there's a bill of
five hundred—and now, madam—   140

LADY TOWNLY.

And now, my lord, down to the ground I thank you.—
(*Aside.*) Now am I convinced, were I weak enough to

125–126. *she can't be sued for*] because debts incurred by a wife
must be recovered from her husband.

139. *bill*] a written order for money, drawn on an individual or
business firm, and payable to the bearer.

love this man I should never get a single guinea from
him.

LORD TOWNLY.

If it be no offense, madam—   145

LADY TOWNLY.

Say what you please, my lord. I am in that harmony of
spirits, it is impossible to put me out of humor.

LORD TOWNLY.

How long, in reason then, do you think that sum ought
to last you?

LADY TOWNLY.

Oh my dear, dear lord, now you have spoiled all again! 150
How is it possible I should answer for an event that so
utterly depends upon Fortune? But to show you that I
am more inclined to get money than to throw it away—
I have a strong possession that with this five hundred,
I shall win five thousand.   155

LORD TOWNLY.

Madam, if you were to win ten thousand, it would be
no satisfaction to me.

LADY TOWNLY.

Oh, the churl! Ten thousand! What, not so much as
wish I might win ten thousand? Ten thousand, oh, the
charming sum! What infinite pretty things might a   160
woman of spirit do, with ten thousand guineas! O' my
conscience, if she were a woman of true spirit—she—she
might lose 'em all again!

LORD TOWNLY.

And I had rather it should be so, madam, provided I
could be sure that were the last you would lose.   165

LADY TOWNLY.

Well my lord, to let you see I design to play all the good
housewife I can: I am now going to a party at quadrille,
only to piddle with a little of it, at poor two guineas a

---

154. *possession*] conviction.
167. *quadrille*] a card game for four players, being a French version
of ombre. By the end of 1724 quadrille was "all the mode" in London
(Mrs. Delany, vol. I, p. 102).
168. *piddle*] trifle, toy.

fish, with the Duchess of Quiteright.   *Exit* Lady Townly.

LORD TOWNLY.

Insensible creature! Neither reproaches or indulgence, 170
kindness or severity, can wake her to the least reflection.
Continual license has lulled her into such a lethargy of
care that she speaks of her excesses with the same easy
confidence as if they were so many virtues. What a turn
has her head taken! But how to cure it? I am afraid the 175
physic must be strong, that reaches her; lenitives, I see,
are to no purpose. Take my friends' opinion; Manly will
speak freely, my sister with tenderness to both sides.
They know my case; I'll talk with 'em.

Enter a Servant

SERVANT.

Mr. Manly, my lord, has sent to know if your lordship 180
was at home.

LORD TOWNLY.

They did not deny me?

SERVANT.

No, my lord.

LORD TOWNLY.

Very well; step up to my sister, and say I desire to speak
with her.   185

SERVANT.

Lady Grace is here, my lord.   *Exit* Servant.

Enter Lady Grace.

LORD TOWNLY.

So, lady fair, what pretty weapon have you been killing
your time with?

LADY GRACE.

A huge folio, that has almost killed me. I think I have
half read my eyes out.   190

---

169. *fish*] a bone or ivory counter, shaped like a fish, and representing an agreed sum of money. At ombre and quadrille each player
lays down one *fish* as his initial stake.
172–173. *lethargy of care*] insensibility to all serious matters.
176. *lenitives*] soothing medicines.
182. *deny me*] "say that I was not at home"—the usual method of
keeping out unwanted visitors.

LORD TOWNLY.

Oh, you should not pore so much just after dinner, child.

LADY GRACE.

That's true, but anybody's thoughts are better than always one's own, you know.

LORD TOWNLY.

Who's there?

Enter Servant.

Leave word at the door, I am at home to nobody but 195
Mr. Manly.   [*Exit* Servant.]

LADY GRACE.

And why is *he* excepted, pray my lord?

LORD TOWNLY.

I hope, madam, you have no objection to his company?

LADY GRACE.

Your particular orders, upon my being here, look indeed
as if you thought I had not.   200

LORD TOWNLY.

And your ladyship's inquiry into the reason of those
orders, shows at least it was not a matter indifferent to
you.

LADY GRACE.

Lord, you make the oddest constructions, brother!

LORD TOWNLY.

Look you, my grave Lady Grace; in one serious word—I 205
wish you had him.

LADY GRACE.

I can't help that.

LORD TOWNLY.

Hah, you can't help it! Ha ha! The flat simplicity of
that reply was admirable.

LADY GRACE.

Pooh, you tease one, brother.   210

LORD TOWNLY.

Come, I beg pardon, child. This is not a point, I grant

202. shows] *1735*; show *01–3*.

194. *Who's there*] "Who is at hand?"—the customary formula for
summoning a servant.

you, to trifle upon; therefore I hope you'll give me
leave to be serious.

LADY GRACE.

If you desire it, brother; though upon my word, as to
Mr. Manly's having any serious thoughts of me—I know   215
nothing of it.

LORD TOWNLY.

Well, there's nothing wrong in your making a doubt of
it. But in short—I find, by his conversation of late, he
has been looking round the world for a wife; and if
you were to look round the world for a husband, he's   220
the first man I would give to you.

LADY GRACE.

Then whenever he makes me any offer, brother, I will
certainly tell you of it.

LORD TOWNLY.

Oh, that's the last thing he'll do. He'll never make you
an offer, till he's pretty sure it won't be refused.   225

LADY GRACE.

Now you make me curious. Pray, did he ever make any
offer of that kind to you?

LORD TOWNLY.

Not directly—but that imports nothing. He is a man too
well acquainted with the female world to be brought into
a high opinion of any one woman, without some well- 230
examined proof of her merit. Yet I have reason to believe
that your good sense, your turn of mind, and your way
of life have brought him to so favorable a one of you,
that a few days will reduce him to talk plainly to me;
which as yet (notwithstanding our friendship) I have 235
neither declined, nor encouraged him to.

LADY GRACE.

I am mighty glad we are so near in our way of thinking,
for to tell you the truth he is much upon the same
terms with me. You know he has a satirical turn, but
never lashes any folly without giving due encomiums to 240
its opposite virtue; and upon such occasions he is sometimes particular, in turning his compliments upon *me*,
which I don't receive with any reserve lest he should
imagine I take them to myself.

LORD TOWNLY.

You are right, child. When a man of merit makes his 245
addresses, good sense may give him an answer, without
scorn or coquetry.

LADY GRACE.

Hush, he's here.

Enter Mr. Manly.

MANLY.

My lord, your most obedient.

LORD TOWNLY.

Dear Manly, yours. I was thinking to send to you.   250

MANLY.

Then I am glad I am here, my lord. —Lady Grace, I kiss
your hands. What, only you two? How many visits may
a man make, before he falls into such unfashionable company! A brother and sister soberly sitting at home, when
the whole town is a-gadding! I question if there is so 255
particular a *tête-à-tête* again, in the whole parish of
St. James's.

LADY GRACE.

Fie, fie, Mr. Manly, how censorious you are!

MANLY.

I had not made the reflection, madam, but that I saw you
an exception to it. —Where's my lady?   260

LORD TOWNLY.

That I believe is impossible to guess.

MANLY.

Then I won't try, my lord—

LORD TOWNLY.

But 'tis probable I may hear of her, by that time I have
been four or five hours in bed.

MANLY.

Now if that were my case, I believe I should—but I beg 265
pardon, my lord.

---

256. *again*] anywhere else.
257. *St. James's*] at the time the most fashionable residential dis-
trict in London, immediately to the north and east of St. James's
Palace.

LORD TOWNLY.

Indeed sir, you shall not. You will oblige me if you speak out, for it was upon this head I wanted to see you.

MANLY.

Why then my lord, since you oblige me to proceed: if that were my case—I believe I should certainly sleep in 270
another house.

LADY GRACE.

How do you mean?

MANLY.

Only a compliment, madam.

LADY GRACE.

A compliment?

MANLY.

Yes madam, in rather turning myself out of doors than 275
her.

LADY GRACE.

Don't you think that would be going too far?

MANLY.

I don't know but it might, madam, for in strict justice I
think she ought rather to go, than I.

LADY GRACE.

This is new doctrine, Mr. Manly.   280

MANLY.

As old, madam, as "Love, honor, and obey." When a
woman will stop at nothing that's wrong, why should a
man balance anything that's right?

LADY GRACE.

Bless me, but this is fomenting things—

MANLY.

Fomentations, madam, are sometimes necessary to dispel 285
tumors—though I don't directly advise my lord to do this.
This is only what, upon the same provocation, I would
do myself.

LADY GRACE.

Aye, aye, *you* would do! Bachelors' wives, indeed, are
finely governed.   290

---

283. *balance*] place in the opposite scale.
289–290. *Bachelors'* . . . *governed*] a shortened form of the proverb
"Bachelors' wives and maids' children are well taught."

MANLY.

If the married men's were as well, I am apt to think we
should not see so many mutual plagues taking the air,
in separate coaches.

LADY GRACE.

Well, but suppose it your own case. Would you part
with a wife because she now and then stays out, in the 295
best company?

LORD TOWNLY.

Well said, Lady Grace. Come, stand up for the privilege
of your sex. This is like to be a warm debate. I shall
edify.

MANLY.

Madam, I think a wife, after midnight, has no occasion 300
to be in better company than her husband's; and that
frequent unreasonable hours make the best company—the
worst company she can fall into.

LADY GRACE.

But if people of condition are to keep company with one
another, how is it possible to be done, unless one con- 305
forms to their hours?

MANLY.

I can't find that any woman's good breeding obliges her
to conform to other people's vices.

LORD TOWNLY.

I doubt, child, here we are got a little on the wrong side
of the question.   310

LADY GRACE.

Why so, my lord? I can't think the case so bad as Mr.
Manly states it. People of quality are not tied down to
the rules of those who have their fortunes to make.

MANLY.

No people, madam, are above being tied down to some
rules, that have fortunes to lose.   315

---

292. *mutual plagues*] an echo of Vanbrugh's *Provoked Wife:* "lest
your mutual plagues should make you both run mad . . ." (V.v.229–230).
    309. *I doubt*] I'm afraid, I suppose (as frequently elsewhere in this
play).

LADY GRACE.

Pooh! I'm sure if you were to take my side of the argument you would be able to say something more for it.

LORD TOWNLY.

Well, what say you to that, Manly?

MANLY.

Why troth, my lord, I have something to say.

LADY GRACE.

Aye, that I should be glad to hear now!   320

LORD TOWNLY.

Out with it.

MANLY.

Then in one word, this, my lord: I have often thought that the misconduct of my lady has, in a great measure, been owing to your lordship's treatment of her.

LADY GRACE.

Bless me!   325

LORD TOWNLY.

My treatment?

MANLY.

Aye my lord, you so idolized her before marriage that you even indulged her, like a mistress, after it. In short, you continued the lover, when you should have taken up the husband.   330

LADY GRACE.

Oh frightful, this is worse than t'other! Can a husband love a wife too well?

MANLY.

As easily, madam, as a wife may love her husband too little.

LORD TOWNLY.

So, you two are never like to agree, I find.   335

LADY GRACE.

Don't be positive, brother.— (*Aside.*) I am afraid we are both of a mind already. —And do you, at this rate, ever hope to be married, Mr. Manly?

333. her] *03*; a *01–2*.

MANLY.

Never, madam—till I can meet with a woman that likes
my doctrine.   340

LADY GRACE.

'Tis pity but your mistress should hear it.

MANLY.

Pity me, madam, when I marry the woman that won't
hear it.

LADY GRACE (aside).

I think at least he can't say that's me.

MANLY.

And so, my lord, by giving her more power than was 345
needful, she has none where she wants it; having such
entire possession of you, she is not mistress of herself.
And, mercy on us, how many fine women's heads have
been turned upon the same occasion!

LORD TOWNLY.

Oh Manly, 'tis too true; there's the source of my dis- 350
quiet. She knows and has abused her power. Nay, I am
still so weak (with shame I speak it), 'tis not an hour ago
that in the midst of my impatience—I gave her another
bill for five hundred, to throw away.

MANLY.

Well my lord, to let you see I am sometimes upon the 355
side of good nature, I won't absolutely blame you; for
the greater your indulgence, the more you have to reproach her with.

LADY GRACE.

Aye Mr. Manly, here now I begin to come in with you.
Who knows, my lord, you may have a good account of 360
your kindness!

MANLY.

That, I am afraid, we had not best depend upon. But
since you have had so much patience, my lord, even go
on with it a day or two more; and upon her ladyship's
next sally, be a little rounder in your expostulation. If 365

341. 'Tis pity . . . hear it] "What a good thing it would be if your
doctrine were to come to your mistress' ears."
360. account] profitable result, advantage.

that don't work, drop her some cool hints of a determined reformation, and leave her—to breakfast upon 'em.

LORD TOWNLY.

You are perfectly right. How valuable is a friend, in our
anxiety!

MANLY.

Therefore to divert that, my lord, I beg for the present 370
we may call another cause.

LADY GRACE.

Aye, for goodness' sake let's have done with this.

LORD TOWNLY.

With all my heart.

LADY GRACE.

Have you no news abroad, Mr. Manly?

MANLY.

Apropos, I have some, madam; and I believe, my lord, 375
as extraordinary in its kind—

LORD TOWNLY.

Pray, let's have it.

MANLY.

Do you know that your country neighbor, and my wise
kinsman, Sir Francis Wronghead, is coming to town with
his whole family? 380

LORD TOWNLY.

The fool! What can be his business here?

MANLY.

Oh, of the last importance, I'll assure you—no less than
the business of the nation.

LORD TOWNLY.

Explain.

MANLY.

He has carried his election, against Sir John Worthland. 385

LORD TOWNLY.

The deuce! What, for—for—

MANLY.

The famous borough of Guzzledown.

---

371. *call another cause*] change the subject.
380. *family*] the entire household, including servants.

LORD TOWNLY.

A proper representative, indeed.

LADY GRACE.

Pray Mr. Manly, don't I know him?

MANLY.

You have dined with him, madam, when I was last down 390
with my lord at Bellmont.

LADY GRACE.

Was not that he, that got a little merry before dinner,
and overset the tea table in making his compliments to
my lady?

MANLY.

The same.   395

LADY GRACE.

Pray what are his circumstances? I know but very little
of him.

MANLY.

Then he is worth your knowing, I can tell you, madam.
His estate, if clear, I believe might be a good two thousand pound a year; though as it was left him, saddled 400
with two jointures, and two weighty mortgages upon it,
there is no saying what it is. But that he might be sure
never to mend it, he married a profuse young hussy, for
love, without ever a penny of money. Thus having, like
his brave ancestors, provided heirs for the family (for his 405
dove breeds like a tame pigeon) he now finds children
and interest-money make such a bawling about his ears,
that at last he has taken the friendly advice of his kinsman, the good Lord Danglecourt, to run his estate two
thousand pound more in debt, to put the whole man- 410
agement of what's left into Paul Pillage's hands, that he
may be at leisure himself to retrieve his affairs by being
a Parliament-man.

---

391. *Bellmont*] Lord Townly's country house.

401. *jointures*] A *jointure* is part of the husband's estate which is
settled on his wife at marriage as a security in the event of her being
widowed. It usually takes the form of an annuity.

411. *Paul Pillage*] presumably the steward of the Wronghead estate;
estate stewards in general had acquired a reputation for feathering
their own nests.

LORD TOWNLY.

A most admirable scheme, indeed!

MANLY.

And with this politic prospect, he's now upon his   415
journey to London.

LORD TOWNLY.

What can it end in?

MANLY.

Pooh, a journey into the country again.

LORD TOWNLY.

Do you think he'll stir till his money's gone, or at least
till the session is over?   420

MANLY.

If my intelligence is right, my lord, he won't sit long
enough to give his vote for a turnpike.

LORD TOWNLY.

How so?

MANLY.

Oh, a bitter business! He had scarce a vote in the whole
town, beside the returning officer. Sir John will certainly   425
have it heard at the bar of the House, and send him
about his business again.

LORD TOWNLY.

Then he has made a fine business of it, indeed.

MANLY.

Which, as far as my little interest will go, shall be done
in as few days as possible.   430

LADY GRACE.

But why would you ruin the poor gentleman's fortune,
Mr. Manly?

---

422. *turnpike*] In the 1720s numerous acts were introduced to set
up turnpikes, or toll-barriers, with a view to improving road com-
munications; such acts were routine (and swiftly dispatched) pieces of
Parliamentary business.

425. *returning officer*] the official presiding at elections. He was
empowered (and might be bribed) to refuse electors the right to vote.

426. *have it heard . . . House*] The *bar* of the House of Commons
was a wooden rail facing the Speaker's chair. Petitions alleging corrupt
and wrongful election were normally presented there.

MANLY.

No, madam, I would only spoil his project, to save his
fortune.

LADY GRACE.

How are you concerned enough to do either?   435

MANLY.

Why, I have some obligations to the family, madam. I
enjoy at this time a pretty estate which Sir Francis was
heir at law to; but, by his being a booby, the last will
of an obstinate old uncle gave it me.

Enter a Servant.

SERVANT (*to* Manly).

Sir, here's one of your servants from your house desires   440
to speak with you.

MANLY.

Will you give him leave to come in, my lord?

LORD TOWNLY.

Sir, the ceremony's of your own making.   [*Exit* Servant.]

Enter [James,] *Manly's servant.*

MANLY.

Well, James, what's the matter now?

JAMES.

Sir, here's John Moody's just come to town. He says Sir   445
Francis, and all the family, will be here tonight, and is
in a great hurry to speak with you.

MANLY.

Where is he?

JAMES.

At our house, sir. He has been gaping and stumping
about the streets in his dirty boots, and asking everyone 450
he meets if they can tell him where he may have a good
lodging for a Parliament-man, till he can hire a handsome whole house, fit for all his family, for the winter.

MANLY.

I am afraid, my lord, I must wait upon Mr. Moody.

LORD TOWNLY.

Prithee, let's have him here; he will divert us.   455

MANLY.

Oh my lord, he's such a cub! Not but he's so near common sense that he passes for a wit in the family.

LADY GRACE.

I beg, of all things, we may have him. I am in love with
Nature, let her dress be never so homely.

MANLY.

Then desire him to come hither, James.   460

Exit James.

LADY GRACE.

Pray what may be Mr. Moody's post?

MANLY.

Oh, his *maître d'hôtel*, his butler, his bailiff, his hind,
his huntsman, and sometimes—his companion.

LORD TOWNLY.

It runs in my head, that the moment this knight has set
him down in the House, he will get up, to give them the   465
earliest proof of what importance he is to the public in
his own county.

MANLY.

Yes, and when they have heard him he will find that his
utmost importance stands valued at—sometimes being
invited to dinner.   470

LADY GRACE.

And her ladyship, I suppose, will make as considerable
a figure in her sphere too.

MANLY.

That you may depend upon. For (if I don't mistake) she
has ten times more of the jade in her than she yet
knows of; and she will so improve in this rich soil, in   475
a month, that she will visit all the ladies that will let
her into their houses, and run in debt to all the shop-
keepers that will let her into their books. In short,
before her important spouse has made five pounds by his
eloquence at Westminster, she will have lost five hun-   480
dred at dice and quadrille in the parish of St. James's.

464–465. *set him down*] taken his seat as a newly-elected Member of
Parliament.

LORD TOWNLY.

So that by that time he is declared unduly elected, a
swarm of duns will be ready for their money, and his
worship—will be ready for a jail.

MANLY.

Yes, yes, that I reckon will close the account of this 485
hopeful journey to London. —But see, here comes the
forehorse of the team.

Enter John Moody.

Oh, honest John!

JOHN MOODY.

Ad's waunds and heart, Master Manly, I'm glad I ha'
fun' ye. Lawd, lawd, give me a buss! Why, that's friendly 490
naw. Flesh, I thought we should never ha' got hither.
Well, and how d'ye do, master? —Good lack, I beg pardon
for my bawldness. I did not see 'at his honor was here.

LORD TOWNLY.

Mr. Moody, your servant. I am glad to see you in
London. I hope all the good family is well.   495

JOHN MOODY.

Thanks be praised, your honor, they are all in pretty
good heart, thof we have had a power of crosses upo'
th' road.

LADY GRACE.

I hope my lady has had no hurt, Mr. Moody.

JOHN MOODY.

Noa, and please your ladyship, she was never in better 500
humor; there's money enough stirring now.

MANLY.

What has been the matter, John?

---

482. *unduly*] improperly—so that the election is void.
489. *Ad's waunds*] "(By) God's wounds." Cf. *Ad's wauntlikins,* **IV,**
158–159.
490. *fun'*] found.
492. *Good lack*] an exclamation of surprise and apology.
497. *thof*] a variant of "though" in rustic and uneducated speech.
500. *and . . . ladyship*] if your ladyship pleases. *And* (or more often
an') meaning "if" was current in many dialects, and is liberally used
in this play.

JOHN MOODY.

> Why, we came up in such a hurry (you mun think), that
> our tackle was not so tight as it should be.

MANLY.

> Come, tell us all. Pray how do they travel?　　　　　505

JOHN MOODY.

> Why i' th'awld coach, master; and 'cause my lady loves
> to do things handsome, to be sure, she would have a
> couple of cart-horses clapped to th' four old geldings,
> that neighbors might see she went up to London in her
> coach and six. And so Giles Joulter the plowman rides 510
> postilion.

MANLY (aside).

> Very well! The journey sets out as it should do. —What,
> do they bring all the children with them too?

JOHN MOODY.

> Noa, noa, only the younk squoire, and Miss Jenny. The
> other foive are all out at board, at half-a-crown a head a 515
> week, with Joan Grouse, at Smoke-dunghill Farm.

MANLY.

> Good again! A right English academy for younger chil-
> dren!

JOHN MOODY (not understanding him).

> Anon, sir?

LADY GRACE.

> Poor souls, what will become of 'em?　　　　　520

JOHN MOODY.

> Nay, nay, for that matter, madam, they are in very good
> hands. Joan loves 'um an' as thof they were all her own,
> for she was wet-nurse to every mother's babe of 'um. Aye,
> aye, they'll ne'er want for a bellyful there.

520–525. Poor souls . . . simpli-
city] *01, 03*; om. *02.*

---

503. *mun*] must (northern and midland dialects).
510. *Joulter*] A *joulter-head* is a blockhead, so Giles's surname indi-
cates clumsiness and stupidity.
519. *Anon*] an exclamation of puzzlement, "implying that the auditor
has failed to catch the speaker's words or meaning" *(OED).*

THE PROVOKED HUSBAND I.

LADY GRACE.

What simplicity! 525

MANLY.

The lud 'a mercy upon all good folks! What work will these people make! *Holding up his hands.*

LORD TOWNLY.

And when do you expect them here, John?

JOHN MOODY.

Why we were in hopes to ha' come yesterday, an' it had no' been that th'owld wheaze-belly horse tired. And then 530 we were so cruelly loaden that the two fore-wheels came crash! down at once, in Waggonrut Lane, and there we lost four hours afore we could set things to rights again.

MANLY.

So they bring all their baggage with the coach, then?

JOHN MOODY.

Aye, aye, and good store on't there is. Why, my lady's 535 gear alone were as much as filled four portmantel trunks, beside the great deal box that heavy Ralph and the monkey sit upon behind.

LORD TOWNLY. LADY GRACE. MANLY.

Ha, ha, ha!

LADY GRACE.

Well Mr. Moody, and pray how many are they within 540 the coach?

JOHN MOODY.

Why there's my lady, and his worship, and the younk squoire, and Miss Jenny, and the fat lap dog, and my lady's maid, Mrs. Handy, and Doll Tripe the cook, that's all—only Doll puked a little with riding backwards, so 545 they hoisted her into the coach box, and then her stomach was easy.

LADY GRACE.

Oh, I see 'em, I see 'em go by me. Ah ha! *Laughing.*

526–527. *What work . . . make*] "To make (a) work" is to cause trouble, to create havoc.

536. *portmantel*] at this date still an acceptable variant of *portmanteau*, though perhaps just beginning to be considered provincial.

538. *monkey*] a fashionable pet, like the lap dog.

546. *coach box*] the driver's seat.

—35—

JOHN MOODY.

  Then yow mun think, mester, there was some stowage
  for th' belly, as well as th' back too. Childer are apt to 550
  be famished upo' th' road, so we had such cargoes of
  plum-cake, and baskets of tongues, and biscuits, and
  cheese, and cold boiled beef—and then, in case of sickness, bottles of cherry-brandy, plague-water, sack, tent,
  and strong beer so plenty as made th'owld coach crack 555
  again. Mercy upon them, and send 'em all well to town,
  I say.

MANLY.

  Aye, and well out on't again, John.

JOHN MOODY.

  Od's bud, master, you're a wise mon; and for that matter
  so am I. Whoam's whoam, I say. I'm sure we ha' got but 560
  little good, e'er sin' we turned our backs on't. Nothing
  but mischief! Some devil's trick or other plagued us,
  aw th' dey lung. Crack! goes one thing, bawnce! goes
  another. "Woa!" says Roger—then sowse! we are all set
  fast in a slough. "Whaw!" cries Miss; scream go the maids, 565
  and bawl just as an' thof they were stuck. And so, mercy
  on us, this was the trade from morning to night. But
  my lady was in such murrain haste to be here, that set

---

  550. *th' belly . . . th' back*] *Belly* and *back*—standing for food and
clothing—keep each other company in several proverbs.
  550. *Childer*] a northern variant of "children."
  554. *plague-water*] "an infusion of various herbs and roots in spirits
of wine, of supposed efficacy against the plague" *(OED)*.
  554. *sack*] Spanish white wine; an unfashionable, country gentleman's drink.
  554. *tent*] a dark red Spanish wine *(vino tinto)*; it was not very
alcoholic.
  559. *Od's bud*] This, like its variants *s'bud(s)* and *(Od)'s bodikins*,
is a corruption of the oath "By God's body."
  560. *Whoam's whoam*] Home's home.
  563. *aw th' dey lung*] all the day long.
  566. *stuck*] a Moodyesque joke; they are stuck fast in the mud, and
screaming like "stuck" pigs.
  568. *murrain*] A *murrain* is an infectious cattle disease; so "plaguy,
confounded."

out she would, thof I tould her it was Childermas Day.

MANLY.

These ladies, these ladies, John—   570

JOHN MOODY.

Ah, measter, I ha' seen a little of 'em; and I find that
the best, when she's mended, won't ha' much goodness
to spare.

LORD TOWNLY.

Well said, John. Ha ha!

MANLY.

I hope at least, you and your good woman agree still.   575

JOHN MOODY.

Aye, aye, much of a muchness. Bridget sticks to me,
though as for her goodness—why, she was willing to come
to London too. "But hawld a bit! No, noa," says I,
"there may be mischief enough done, without you."

MANLY.

Why that was bravely spoken, John, and like a man.   580

JOHN MOODY.

Ah, weast heart, were measter but hawf the mon that
I am. Od's wookers! thof he'll speak stawtly too sometimes. But then he conno' hawld it—no, he conno' hawld
it.

LORD TOWNLY. LADY GRACE. MANLY.

Ha, ha, ha!   585

JOHN MOODY.

Od's flesh, but I mun hie me whoam. Th' cooach will
be coming every hour naw. But measter charged me to

575–585. I hope . . . Ha, ha, ha] 577. her] _03_; _om. 01._
_01, 03_; _om. 02._

---

569. _Childermas Day_] the Festival of the Holy Innocents, celebrated
on December 28. If the festival fell, say, on a Monday, then by
extension every Monday throughout the year was known as Childermas
Day. It was considered specially unlucky, and a journey begun on
that day was sure not to prosper.

581. _weast heart_] alas, oh dear. A contraction of the northern dialect
phrase _wae's t'heart,_ "woe is to the heart."

582. _Od's wookers_] perhaps a variant of _Od's zookers,_ "God succor
us."

583. _conno' hawld it_] cannot hold it, i.e., cannot maintain his stout
tone.

find your worship out. For he has hugey business with
you, and will certainly wait upon you, by that time he
can put on a clean neckcloth.   590

MANLY.

Oh, John, I'll wait upon him.

JOHN MOODY.

Why you wonno' be so kind, wull ye?

MANLY.

If you'll tell me where you lodge.

JOHN MOODY.

Just i' th' street next to where your worship dwells, the
sign of the Golden Ball—it's gold all over—where they 595
sell ribands, and flappits, and other sort of gear for
gentlewomen.

MANLY.

A milliner's?

JOHN MOODY.

Aye, aye, one Mrs. Motherly's. Waunds, she has a couple
of clever girls there a-stitching i' th' fore-room.   600

MANLY.

Yes, yes, she is a woman of good business, no doubt
on't. Who recommended that house to you, John?

JOHN MOODY.

The greatest good fortune in the world, sure! For as I
was gaping about streets, who should look out of the
window there, but the fine gentleman that was always 605
riding by our coach side at York races—Count—Count
Basset, aye, that's he.

599–614. Waunds . . . here in
town] *O1, O3*; om. *O2.*

---

592. *wonno'*] will not.

596. *flappits*] *OED* suggests "little flaps," hence "finery." Or perhaps
a comic conflation of *flap* and *lappet* (a streamer or ribbon attached
to a woman's headdress).

606–607. *Count Basset*] Since Count is not a rank of the English
nobility, we are meant to infer that he has acquired his title on the
Continent. *Basset* is a card game in which bets are laid on upturned
cards. It was regularly played for high stakes, and was therefore
particularly attractive to sharpers.

MANLY.

Basset? Oh, I remember; I know him by sight.

JOHN MOODY.

Well, to be sure, as civil a gentleman to see to—

MANLY (*aside*).

As any sharper in town.   610

JOHN MOODY.

At York, he used to breakfast with my lady every morning.

MANLY (*aside*).

Yes, yes, and I suppose her ladyship will return his compliment here in town.

JOHN MOODY.

Well measter—   615

LORD TOWNLY.

My service to Sir Francis, and my lady, John.

LADY GRACE.

And mine pray, Mr. Moody.

JOHN MOODY.

Ah, your honors, they'll be proud on't, I dare say.

MANLY.

I'll bring my compliments myself. So, honest John—

JOHN MOODY.

Dear Measter Monly, the goodness of goodness bless and 620 preserve you.   *Exit* John Moody.

LORD TOWNLY.

What a natural creature 'tis!

LADY GRACE.

Well, I can't but think John, in a wet afternoon in the country, must be very good company.

LORD TOWNLY.

Oh, the tramontane! If this were known at half the 625 quadrille-tables in town, they would lay down their cards to laugh at you.

LADY GRACE.

And the minute they took them up again, they would do the same at the losers. But to let you see that I

---

609. *to see to*] to look at; in appearance.
625. *tramontane*] uncouth, boorish person.

think good company may sometimes want cards to keep 630
them together, what think you if we three sat soberly
down to kill an hour at ombre?

MANLY.

I shall be too hard for you, madam.

LADY GRACE.

No matter; I shall have as much advantage of my lord,
as you have of me.   635

LORD TOWNLY.

Say you so, madam? Have at you then! [*Calls to a
servant.*]   Here, get the ombre-table and cards.

Exit Lord Townly.

LADY GRACE.

Come, Mr. Manly. I know you don't forgive me now.

MANLY.

I don't know whether I ought to forgive your thinking
so, madam. Where do you imagine I could pass my time 640
so agreeably?

LADY GRACE.

I'm sorry my lord is not here to take his share of the
compliment. But he'll wonder what's become of us.

MANLY.

I'll follow in a moment, madam.   *Exit* Lady Grace.
It must be so. She sees I love her—yet with what un- 645
offending decency she avoids an explanation! How
amiable is every hour of her conduct! What a vile opinion have I had of the whole sex, for these ten years
past, which this sensible creature has recovered in less
than one! Such a companion, sure, might compensate all 650
the irksome disappointments that pride, folly, and false-
hood ever gave me.

> Could women regulate, like her, their lives,
> What halcyon days were in the gift of wives!
> Vain rovers then might envy what they hate,   655
> And only fools would mock the married state.   *Exit.*

642. I'm] *03;* I am *01–2.*

---

632. *ombre*] a card game for three players. It was the most fashionable game in the period 1700–1720, after which it was displaced by
quadrille.

655. *rovers*] libertines, rakes.

ACT II

Scene: Mrs. Motherly's house.
Enter Count Basset *and* Mrs. Motherly.

COUNT BASSET.

    I tell you, there is not such a family in England for you.
Do you think I would have gone out of your lodgings
for anybody that was not sure to make you easy for
the winter?

MRS. MOTHERLY.

    Nay, I see nothing against it sir, but the gentleman's   5
being a Parliament-man; and when people may, as it
were, think one impertinent, or be out of humor, you
know, when a body comes to ask for one's own—

COUNT BASSET.

    Pshah, prithee never trouble thy head—his pay is as
good as the Bank. Why, he has above two thousand   10
pound a year.

MRS. MOTHERLY.

    Alas-a-day, that's nothing. Your people of ten thousand a
year have ten thousand things to do with it.

COUNT BASSET.

    Nay, if you are afraid of being out of your money, what
do you think of going a little with me, Mrs. Motherly?   15

MRS. MOTHERLY.

    As how?

COUNT BASSET.

    Why, I have a game in my hand, in which, if you'll croup
me—that is help me to play it—you shall go five hundred
to nothing.

MRS. MOTHERLY.

    Say you so? Why then, I go, sir. And now pray let's see   20
your game.

    5–6. *Nay, I see . . . Parliament-man*] Mrs. Motherly would not be
able to sue her tenant for debt, since Members of Parliament enjoyed
immunity from arrest and legal action during a Parliamentary session.

    10. *Bank*] the Bank of England, founded 1694.

    17. *croup*] In the game of basset the croupier assists the dealer or
banker so that he does not overlook "anything which might turn to
his Profit" (Seymour, part I, p. 114).

COUNT BASSET.

Look you, in one word my cards lie thus. When I was down this summer at York, I happened to lodge in the same house with this knight's lady that's now coming to lodge with you.   25

MRS. MOTHERLY.

Did you so, sir?

COUNT BASSET.

And sometimes had the honor to breakfast, and pass an idle hour with her—

MRS. MOTHERLY.

Very good; and here I suppose you would have the impudence to sup, and be busy with her.   30

COUNT BASSET.

Pshah, prithee hear me!

MRS. MOTHERLY.

Is this your game? I would not give sixpence for it. What, you have a passion for her pin money! No, no, country ladies are not so flush of it.

COUNT BASSET.

Nay, if you won't have patience—   35

MRS. MOTHERLY.

One had need have a good deal, I am sure, to hear you talk at this rate. Is this your way of making my poor niece Myrtilla easy?

COUNT BASSET.

Death! I shall do it still, if the woman will but let me speak—   40

MRS. MOTHERLY.

Had not you a letter from her this morning?

COUNT BASSET.

I have it here in my pocket; this is it.

Shows it, and puts it up again.

MRS. MOTHERLY.

Aye, but I don't find you have made any answer to it.

COUNT BASSET.

How the devil can I, if you won't hear me?

MRS. MOTHERLY.

What, hear you talk of another woman?   45

COUNT BASSET.

Oh lud, oh lud! I tell you, I'll make her fortune—'ounds,
I'll marry her.

MRS. MOTHERLY.

A likely matter! If you would not do it when she was
a maid, your stomach is not so sharp-set now, I presume.

COUNT BASSET.

Hey-day, why your head begins to turn, my dear. The   50
devil! You did not think I proposed to marry her myself?

MRS. MOTHERLY.

If you don't, who the devil do you think will marry her?

COUNT BASSET.

Why, a fool—

MRS. MOTHERLY.

Humh, there may be sense in that—

COUNT BASSET.

Very good; one for t'other then. If I can help her to a   55
husband, why should not you come into my scheme of
helping me to a wife?

MRS. MOTHERLY.

Your pardon, sir. Aye, aye, in an honorable affair, you
know, you may command me. But pray where is this
blessed wife and husband to be had?   60

COUNT BASSET.

Now have a little patience. You must know then, this
country knight and his lady bring up in the coach with
them their eldest son, and a daughter, to teach them to—
wash their faces, and turn their toes out.

MRS. MOTHERLY.

Good!   65

COUNT BASSET.

The son is an unlicked whelp, about sixteen, just taken
from school, and begins to hanker after every wench in
the family. The daughter, much of the same age, a pert,
forward hussy, who having eight thousand pound left her

---

49. *sharp-set*] literally "hungry"; hence "eager, lustful."
64. *turn their toes out*] Correct deportment was taught by the
dancing master; when standing, walking, or dancing the toes had to
be kept pointing outwards.

by an old doting grandmother, seems to have a devilish   70
mind to be doing, in her way too.

MRS. MOTHERLY.

And your design is—to put her into business for life?

COUNT BASSET.

Look you, in short, Mrs. Motherly, we gentlemen whose
occasional chariots roll only upon the four aces are
liable sometimes, you know, to have a wheel out of   75
order; which, I confess, is so much my case at present
that my dapple greys are reduced to a pair of ambling
chair-men. Now if with your assistance I can whip up this
young jade into a hackney coach, I may chance in a
day or two after to carry her in my own chariot, *en*   80
famille, to an opera. Now what do you say to me?

MRS. MOTHERLY.

Why, I shall not sleep—for thinking of it. But how will
you prevent the family's smoking your design?

COUNT BASSET.

By renewing my addresses to the mother.

MRS. MOTHERLY.

And how will the daughter like that, think you?   85

COUNT BASSET.

Very well, whilst it covers her own affair.

MRS. MOTHERLY.

That's true, it must do. But, as you say, one for t'other,
sir; I stick to that. If you don't do my niece's business
with the son, I'll blow you with the daughter, depend
upon't.   90

COUNT BASSET.

It's a bet. Pay as we go, I tell you, and the five hundred
shall be staked in a third hand.

MRS. MOTHERLY.

That's honest. —But here comes my niece. Shall we let
her into the secret?

---

74. *chariots*] A chariot was a light four-wheeled carriage for two
passengers, smaller and less stately than a coach.

78. *chair-men*] the bearers of a sedan chair.

83. *smoking*] suspecting.

89. *blow you*] expose you, reveal your plot.

91. *as we go*] according to the way things turn out.

COUNT BASSET.

Time enough! Maybe I may touch upon it.   95

Enter Myrtilla.

MRS. MOTHERLY.

So, niece, are all the rooms done out, and the beds
sheeted?

MYRTILLA.

Yes madam, but Mr. Moody tells us the lady always burns
wax in her own chamber, and we have none in the
house.   100

MRS. MOTHERLY.

Odso, then I must beg your pardon, Count. This is a
busy time you know.   *Exit* Mrs. Motherly.

COUNT BASSET.

Myrtilla, how dost thou do, child?

MYRTILLA.

As well as a losing gamester can.

COUNT BASSET.

Why, what have you lost?   105

MYRTILLA.

What I shall never recover; and what's worse, you that
have won it don't seem to be much the better for't.

COUNT BASSET.

Why child, dost thou ever see anybody overjoyed for
winning a deep stake, six months after it's over?

MYRTILLA.

Would I had never played for it!   110

COUNT BASSET.

Pshah, hang these melancholy thoughts. We may be
friends still.

MYRTILLA.

Dull ones.

COUNT BASSET.

Useful ones, perhaps. Suppose I should help thee to a
good husband?   115

111. Pshah] *1730*; Pshash *01–3*.

---

99. *wax*] Wax candles were considered superior to the coarser and
cheaper kind made of tallow.

MYRTILLA.

I suppose you'll think anyone good enough, that will take me off o' your hands.

COUNT BASSET.

What do you think of the young country squire, the heir of the family that's coming to lodge here?

MYRTILLA.

How should I know what to think of him?   120

COUNT BASSET.

Nay, I only give you the hint, child. It may be worth your while, at least, to look about you. —Hark, what bustle's that without?

Enter Mrs. Motherly *in haste.*

MRS. MOTHERLY.

Sir, sir, the gentleman's coach is at the door; they are all come!   125

COUNT BASSET.

What, already?

MRS. MOTHERLY.

They are just getting out. Won't you step, and lead in my lady? Do you be in the way, niece. I must run and receive them.   *Exit* Mrs. Motherly.

COUNT BASSET.

And think of what I told you.   *Exit* Count. 130

MYRTILLA.

Aye, aye, you have left me enough to think of, as long as I live. A faithless fellow! I am sure, I have been true to him, and for that only reason he wants to be rid of me. And yet 'tis not above six months since, like a merci-less highwayman, he made me deliver all I had in the 135 world. I am sure I begged piteously to save but one poor small bauble. Could I have kept that, I had still kept him; but while women are weak, men will be rogues. And for a bane to both their joys and ours, when our vanity indulges them in such innocent favors as make 140

134–138. And yet . . . kept him]
01–2; om. 03.

128. *Do you . . . way*] be at hand.

them adore us, we can never be well till we grant them the very one that puts an end to their devotion. —But here comes my aunt, and the company.

Mrs. Motherly *returns, showing in* Lady Wronghead *led by* Count Basset.

MRS. MOTHERLY.

If your ladyship pleases to walk into this parlor, madam, only for the present, till your servants have got all your 145 things in.

LADY WRONGHEAD.

Well, dear sir, this is so infinitely obliging. I protest it gives me pain though, to turn you out of your lodging thus.

COUNT BASSET.

No trouble in the least, madam; we single fellows are 150 soon moved. Besides, Mrs. Motherly's my old acquaintance, and I could not be her hindrance.

MRS. MOTHERLY.

The count is so well-bred, madam, I dare say he would do a great deal more, to accommodate your ladyship.

LADY WRONGHEAD.

Oh dear madam!— *(Apart to the* Count.) A good well- 155 bred sort of a woman.

COUNT BASSET.

Oh madam, she is very much among people of quality; she is seldom without them in her house.

LADY WRONGHEAD.

Are there a good many people of quality in this street, Mrs. Motherly? 160

MRS. MOTHERLY.

Now your ladyship is here, madam, I don't believe there is a house without them.

LADY WRONGHEAD.

I am mighty glad of that, for really I think people of quality should always live among one another.

COUNT BASSET.

'Tis what one would choose, indeed, madam. 165

LADY WRONGHEAD.

Bless me, but where are the children all this while?

MRS. MOTHERLY.

Sir Francis, madam, I believe is taking care of them.

SIR FRANCIS *(within)*.

John Moody, stay you by the coach, and see all our
things out. Come, children.

MRS. MOTHERLY.

Here they are, madam.   170

Enter Sir Francis, Squire Richard, *and* Miss Jenny.

SIR FRANCIS.

Well, Count! I mun say it, this was koynd, indeed.

COUNT BASSET.

Sir Francis, give me leave to bid you welcome to London.

SIR FRANCIS.

Pshah, how dost do, mon? Waunds, I'm glad to see thee.
A good sort of a house this!

COUNT BASSET.

Is not that Master Richard?   175

SIR FRANCIS.

Ey, ey, that's young hopeful. —Why dost not baw, Dick?

SQUIRE RICHARD.

So I do, feyther.

COUNT BASSET.

Sir, I am glad to see you. —I protest Mrs. Jane is grown
so, I should not have known her.

SIR FRANCIS.

Come forward, Jenny.   180

JENNY.

Sure, papa, do you think I don't know how to behave
myself?

COUNT BASSET.

If I have permission to approach her, Sir Francis—

JENNY.

Lord, sir, I am in such a frightful pickle—   *Salute.*

---

178. *Mrs.*] The word *Mistress* was used when addressing either an
unmarried girl or a married woman; the abbreviated form *Mrs.* was
almost certainly pronounced "mistress" rather than "missus."

184. *pickle*] untidy state (of dress).

184. S.D. *Salute*] It was customary, on being introduced to a lady,
to kiss her on the lips.

COUNT BASSET.

Every dress that's proper must become you, madam; 185
you have been a long journey.

JENNY.

I hope you will see me in a better, tomorrow, sir.

> Lady Wronghead *whispers* Mrs. Motherly,
> *pointing to* Myrtilla.

MRS. MOTHERLY.

Only a niece of mine, madam, that lives with me. She
will be proud to give your ladyship any assistance in her
power.   190

LADY WRONGHEAD.

A pretty sort of a young woman. —Jenny, you two must
be acquainted.

JENNY.

Oh mamma, I am never strange in a strange place.

> *Salutes* Myrtilla.

MYRTILLA.

You do me a great deal of honor, madam. Madam, your
ladyship's welcome to London.   195

JENNY.

Mamma, I like her prodigiously; she called me "my
ladyship."

SQUIRE RICHARD.

Pray mother, maun't I be acquainted with her too?

LADY WRONGHEAD.

You, you clown! Stay till you learn a little more breeding
first.   200

SIR FRANCIS.

Od's heart, my Lady Wronghead, why do you balk the
lad? How should he ever learn breeding if he does not
put himself forward?

SQUIRE RICHARD.

Why aye, feather, does mother think 'at I'd be uncivil
to her?   205

187. a] *O1–2; om. O3.*

---

193. *never strange*] never unfriendly or reserved. The whole phrase
has a proverbial ring but does not seem to be recorded as a proverb.

-49-

MYRTILLA.

Master has so much good humor, madam, he would soon
gain upon anybody.   *He kisses* Myrtilla.

SQUIRE RICHARD.

Lo' you theere, moather. And yow would but be quiet,
she and I should do well enough.

LADY WRONGHEAD.

Why how now, sirrah! Boys must not be so familiar.   210

SQUIRE RICHARD.

Why, an' I know nobody, haw the murrain mun I pass
my time here, in a strange place? Naw you, and I, and
sister, forsooth, sometimes, in an afternoon, may play
at one and thirty bone-ace, purely.

JENNY.

Speak for yourself, sir. D'ye think I play at such clownish 215
games?

SQUIRE RICHARD.

Why, and you woan't, yo' ma' let it aloane. Then she,
and I, mayhap, will have a bawt at all fours, without you.

SIR FRANCIS.

Noa, noa, Dick, that won't do neither; you mun learn
to make one at ombre, here, child.   220

MYRTILLA.

If master pleases, I'll show it him.

SQUIRE RICHARD.

What, th' Humber? Hoy-day! Why, does our river run
to this tawn, feather?

---

213. *forsooth*] madam. After 1660 *forsooth* was increasingly felt to
be a provincial or "low" term of address. It is used, for example, by
Ben in Congreve's *Love for Love*. (See Susie I. Tucker, " 'Forsooth,
Madam,' " *Notes and Queries*, n.s. IX [1962], 15–16.)

214. *one and thirty bone-ace*] a card game for several players. The
ace of diamonds (called *bone-ace* or *bonne-ace*) is the highest card; the
first player to score thirty-one points is the winner. A "trivial, and very
inconsiderable" game (Seymour, part II, p. 35).

214. *purely*] a colloquial and distinctly "low" expression of pleasure
and approval.

218. *all fours*] a card game for two players; "a Vulgar Game" (Seymour, part II, p. 10).

222. *th' Humber*] Ombre was pronounced "umber"; Squire Richard
knows only the Yorkshire river Humber, formed by the confluence
of the Ouse and the Trent.

SIR FRANCIS.

    Pooh, you silly tony! Ombre is a geam at cards, that
the better sort of people play three together at.   225

SQUIRE RICHARD.

    Nay the moare the merrier, I say. But sister is always
so cross-grained—

JENNY.

    Lord, this boy is enough to deaf people, and one has
really been stuffed up in a coach so long, that—pray
madam, could not I get a little powder for my hair? 230

MYRTILLA.

    If you please to come along with me, madam.

                              Exeunt Myrtilla *and* Jenny.

SQUIRE RICHARD.

    What, has sister ta'en her away naw? Mess, I'll go, and
have a little game with 'em.   *Exit after them.*

LADY WRONGHEAD.

    Well, Count, I hope you won't so far change your lodg-
ing, but you will come and be at home here sometimes? 235

SIR FRANCIS.

    Aye, aye, prithee come and take a bit of mutton with us,
naw and tan, when thou'st nowght to do.

COUNT BASSET.

    Well, Sir Francis, you shall find I'll make but very little
ceremony.

SIR FRANCIS.

    Why aye naw, that's hearty!   240

MRS. MOTHERLY.

    Will your ladyship please to refresh yourself with a dish
of tea, after your fatigue? I think I have pretty good.

LADY WRONGHEAD.

    If you please, Mrs. Motherly; but I believe we had best
have it above stairs.

---

    224. *tony*] simpleton.

    228. *deaf*] deafen. The form *to deaf* survives in northern and mid-
land dialects and is here probably intended to suggest Jenny's pro-
vincialism.

    232. *Mess*] "(by the) Mass"; a low oath, favored by Ben in *Love for
Love*.

    237. *naw and tan*] now and then.

MRS. MOTHERLY.

Very well, madam; it shall be ready immediately.   245

Exit Mrs. Motherly.

LADY WRONGHEAD [*to* Count Basset].

Won't you walk up, sir?

SIR FRANCIS.

Moody!

COUNT BASSET.

Shan't we stay for Sir Francis, madam?

LADY WRONGHEAD.

Lard, don't mind him. He will come, if he likes it.

SIR FRANCIS.

Aye, aye, ne'er heed me, I ha' things to look after. 250

Exeunt Lady Wronghead *and* Count Basset.

Enter John Moody.

JOHN MOODY.

Did your worship want muh?

SIR FRANCIS.

Aye, is the coach cleared, and all our things in?

JOHN MOODY.

Aw but a few bandboxes, and the nook that's left o' th'
goose poy. But a plague on him, th' monkey has gin
us the slip, I think. I suppose he's goan to see his rela- 255
tions, for here looks to be a power of 'um in this tawn—
but heavy Ralph is skawered after him.

SIR FRANCIS.

Why let him go to the devil! No matter and the hawnds
had had him a month ago. But I wish the coach and
horses were got safe to th' inn. This is a sharp tawn; we 260
mun look about us here, John. Therefore I would have
you goa alung with Roger, and see that nobody runs
away with them before they get to the stable.

JOHN MOODY.

Alas-a-day, sir, I believe our awld cattle woan't yeasily

---

251. *muh*] me.
253. *nook*] piece, fragment.
257. *skawered*] To *scour* is to run hurriedly or hastily.
264. *yeasily*] easily.

be run away with tonight. But howsomdever, we'st ta' the 265
best care we can of 'um, poor sawls.

SIR FRANCIS.

Well, well, make haste then.   Moody *goes out, and returns.*

JOHN MOODY.

Od's flesh, here's Measter Monly come to wait upo' your
worship.

SIR FRANCIS.

Wheere is he?   270

JOHN MOODY.

Just coming in, at threshold.

SIR FRANCIS.

Then goa about your business.   *Exit* Moody.

Enter Manly.

Cousin Monly! Sir, I am your very humble servant.

MANLY.

I heard you were come, Sir Francis, and—

SIR FRANCIS.

Od's heart, this was so kindly done of you, naw!   275

MANLY.

I wish you may think it so, cousin, for I confess I
should have been better pleased to have seen you in
any other place.

SIR FRANCIS.

How soa, sir?

MANLY.

Nay, 'tis for your own sake. I'm not concerned.   280

SIR FRANCIS.

Look you cousin; thof I know you wish me well, yet I
don't question I shall give you such weighty reasons for
what I have done that you will say, sir, this is the wisest
journey that ever I made in my life.

---

265. *howsomdever*] north midlands variant of *howsomever* (used
later by Sir Francis) which is a more widespread dialect form of
however.

265. *we'st ta'*] we shall take. The verb-ending *-st* (representing *shall*
or *will*) is a feature of some northern dialects, especially those of Yorkshire. Cf. l. 587, below.

MANLY.

> I think it ought to be, cousin, for I believe you will find 285
> it the most expensive one. Your election did not cost
> you a trifle, I suppose.

SIR FRANCIS.

> Why aye, it's true; that—that did lick a little. But if a
> man's wise (and I han't fawnd yet that I'm a fool)
> there are ways, cousin, to lick oneself whole again.   290

MANLY.

> Nay if you have that secret—

SIR FRANCIS.

> Don't you be fearful, cousin. You'll find that I know
> something.

MANLY.

> If it be anything for your good, I should be glad to know
> it too.   295

SIR FRANCIS.

> In short then, I have a friend in a corner that has let
> me a little into what's what, at Westminster. That's one
> thing.

MANLY.

> Very well, but what good is that to do you?

SIR FRANCIS.

> Why not me, as much as it does other folks?   300

MANLY.

> Other people, I doubt, have the advantage of different
> qualifications.

SIR FRANCIS.

> Why aye, there's it naw! You'll say that I have lived all
> my days i' th' country. What then? I'm o' th' quorum; I
> have been at sessions, and I have made speeches theere, 305
> aye, and at vestry too, and mayhap they may find here—
> that I have brought my tongue up to town with me. D'ye
> take me, naw?

---

288. *lick*] To *lick* means to beat or thrash; hence to sting or hurt. The election expenses made inroads in Sir Francis's estate.

304. *o' th' quorum*] i.e., a Justice of the Peace.

305. *sessions*] the court of Justices which considered local civil and criminal cases.

306. *vestry*] meeting of parishioners to deal with parochial affairs.

MANLY.

If I take your case right, cousin, I am afraid the first
occasion you will have for your eloquence here will be 310
to show that you have any right to make use of it at all.

SIR FRANCIS.

How d'ye mean?

MANLY.

That Sir John Worthland has lodged a petition against
you.

SIR FRANCIS.

Petition? Why aye, there let it lie. We'll find a way to 315
deal with that, I warrant you. Why you forget, cousin,
Sir John's o' th' wrung side, mon.

MANLY.

I doubt, Sir Francis, that will do you but little service;
for in cases very notorious (which I take yours to be)
there is such a thing as a short day, and dispatching them 320
immediately.

SIR FRANCIS.

With all my heart! The sooner I send him home again,
the better.

MANLY.

And this is the scheme you have laid down to repair
your fortune?   325

SIR FRANCIS.

In one word, cousin, I think it my duty. The Wrongheads
have been a considerable family ever since England
was England; and since the world knows I have talents
wherewithal, they shan't say it's my fault if I don't
make as good a figure as any that ever were at the head 330
on't.

MANLY.

Nay, this project, as you have laid it, will come up to

---

317. *o' th' wrung side*] Sir John Worthland, a politically independent
country gentleman, would have voted with the Opposition. Sir Francis
supports the administration, hoping to profit from his allegiance.
320. *a short day*] a legal phrase denoting an early date for dispatching urgent business.
329. *wherewithal*] besides.

anything your ancestors have done these five hundred
years.

SIR FRANCIS.

And let me alone to work it! Mayhap I haven't told 335
you all, neither.

MANLY.

You astonish me! What, and is it full as practicable
as what you *have* told me?

SIR FRANCIS.

Aye, thof I say it, every whit, cousin. You'll find that
I have more irons i' th' fire than one. I doan't come of a 340
fool's errand.

MANLY.

Very well.

SIR FRANCIS.

In a word, my wife has got a friend at court, as well as
myself, and her dowghter Jenny is naw pretty well
grown up—   345

MANLY (*aside*).

And what in the devil's name would he do with the
dowdy?

SIR FRANCIS.

Naw, if I doan't lay in for a husband for her, mayhap i'
this tawn she may be looking out for herself.

MANLY.

Not unlikely.   350

SIR FRANCIS.

Therefore I have some thoughts of getting her to be
Maid of Honor.

MANLY (*aside*).

Oh, he has taken my breath away! But I must hear him
out. —Pray Sir Francis, do you think her education has
yet qualified her for a court?   355

SIR FRANCIS.

Why, the girl is a little too mettlesome, it's true, but
she has tongue enough; she woan't be dashed. Then she

---

352. *Maid of Honor*] Queen Caroline had six Maids of Honor in
attendance, young ladies of good birth and breeding, and very eligible
matches.

shall learn to daunce forthwith, and that will soon teach
her haw to stond still, you know.

MANLY.

Very well; but when she is thus accomplished, you must 360
still wait for a vacancy.

SIR FRANCIS.

Why I hope one has a good chance for that every day,
cousin. For if I take it right, that's a post that folks are
not more willing to get into, than they are to get out of.
It's like an orange tree, upon that accawnt—it will bear 365
blossoms, and fruit that's ready to drop, at the same time.

MANLY.

Well sir, you best know how to make good your pretensions. But pray where is my lady, and my young
cousins? I should be glad to see them too.

SIR FRANCIS.

She's but just taking a dish of tea with the count, and 370
my landlady. I'll call her dawn.

MANLY.

No, no, if she's engaged I shall call again.

SIR FRANCIS.

Od's heart, but you mun see her naw, cousin. What, the
best friend I have in the world!— (*To a servant without.*)   Here, sweetheart, prithee desire my lady, and the 375
gentleman, to come dawn a bit. Tell her, here's cousin
Manly come to wait upon her.

MANLY.

Pray sir, who may the gentleman be?

SIR FRANCIS.

You mun know him to be sure; why it's Count Basset.

MANLY.

Oh, is it he? Your family will be infinitely happy in 380
his acquaintance.

SIR FRANCIS.

Troth, I think so too. He's the civillest man that ever
I knew in my life. Why, here he would go out of his

367–368. *pretensions*] aspirations, designs—but also, punningly, "un-
warranted and pretentious claims."

own lodging, at an hour's warning, purely to oblige my
family. Was n't that kind, naw?   385

SIR FRANCIS.

Extremely civil.— *(Aside.)* The family is in admirable
hands already.

SIR FRANCIS.

Then my lady likes him hugely. All the time of York
races, she would never be withaut him.

MANLY.

That was happy indeed. And a prudent man, you know,   390
should always take care that his wife may have innocent
company.

SIR FRANCIS.

Why aye, that's it, and I think there could not be such
another.

MANLY.

Why truly, for her purpose, I think not.   395

SIR FRANCIS.

Only naw and tan, he—he stonds a leetle too much upon
ceremony; that's his fault.

MANLY.

Oh never fear, he'll mend that every day.— *(Aside.)*
Mercy on us, what a head he has!

SIR FRANCIS.

So, here they come.   400

Enter Lady Wronghead, Count Basset,
and Mrs. Motherly.

LADY WRONGHEAD.

Cousin Manly, this is infinitely obliging. I am extremely
glad to see you.

MANLY.

Your most obedient servant, madam. I am glad to see
your ladyship look so well, after your journey.

LADY WRONGHEAD.

Why really, coming to London is apt to put a little   405
more life in one's looks.

MANLY.

Yet the way of living here is very apt to deaden the
complexion—and give me leave to tell you, as a friend,

madam, you are come to the worst place in the world
for a good woman to grow better in.   410

LADY WRONGHEAD.

Lord, cousin, how should people ever make any figure in
life, that are always moped up in the country?

COUNT BASSET.

Your ladyship certainly takes the thing in a quite right
light, madam. Mr. Manly, your humble servant—ahem.

MANLY (*aside*).

Familiar puppy. —Sir, your most obedient.— (*Aside.*) I 415
must be civil to the rascal, to cover my suspicion of him.

COUNT BASSET.

Was you at White's this morning, sir?

MANLY.

Yes, sir, I just called in.

COUNT BASSET.

Pray—what—was there anything done there?

MANLY.

Much as usual, sir; the same daily carcasses, and the 420
same crows about them.

COUNT BASSET.

The demoivre baronet had a bloody tumble, yesterday.

MANLY.

I hope, sir, you had your share of him?

COUNT BASSET.

No, faith, I came in when it was all over. I think I just
made a couple of bets with him, took up a cool hundred, 425
and so went to the King's Arms.

---

412. *moped up*] apparently a conflation of *mope* (to be dull and
dejected) and *mewed up* (cooped up, confined).

417. *White's*] the chocolate-house in St. James's Street founded
by Francis White in 1693. It was a resort of the nobility, and was
rapidly becoming an exclusive gaming club, renowned for high play.

422. *The demoivre baronet*] Abraham de Moivre (1667–1754), a
French mathematician who settled in London, was well known for his
work on the laws of chance and probability. His *Doctrine of Chances*,
dealing with dice and card games, appeared in 1718. Cibber is apparently alluding to a habitué of White's who gambled according to an
unsuccessful system. The period had its gaming baronets (e.g., Sir
William Culpeper), but I can offer no certain candidate to fit the joke.

426. *the King's Arms*] a tavern at the Haymarket end of Pall Mall,
frequented by rakes and men about town.

LADY WRONGHEAD (*aside*).

What a genteel, easy manner he has!

MANLY (*aside*).

A very hopeful acquaintance I have made here.

Enter Squire Richard, *with a wet brown paper on his face.*

SIR FRANCIS.

How naw, Dick, what's the matter with thy forehead, lad?

SQUIRE RICHARD.

I ha' getten a knuck upon't.   430

LADY WRONGHEAD.

And how did you come by it, you heedless creature?

SQUIRE RICHARD.

Why I was but running after sister, and t'other young
woman, into a little room just naw; and so with that,
they flapped the door full in my feace, and gave me such
a whurr here—I thowght they had beaten my brains out. 435
So I gut a dab of wet brown paper here, to swage it a
while.

LADY WRONGHEAD.

They served you right enough. Will you never have done
with your horseplay?

SIR FRANCIS.

Pooh, never heed it, lad, it will be well by tomorrow. 440
—The boy has a strong head.

MANLY (*aside*).

Yes truly, his skull seems to be of a comfortable thickness.

SIR FRANCIS.

Come, Dick, here's cousin Manly. —Sir, this is your
godson.   445

LADY WRONGHEAD.

Oh, here's my daughter too.

434. flapped] *03*; slupped *01-2*.

---

434. *flapped*] slammed. The *slupped* of 01-2 (see textual note) is a
dialect form of *slapped*, i.e., shut violently.
435. *whurr*] (northern dialect) a sharp blow.
436. *swage*] assuage, relieve (a dialect form).

Enter Miss Jenny.

SQUIRE RICHARD.

Honored gudfeyther, I crave leave to ask your blessing.

MANLY.

Thou hast it, child—and if it will do thee any good, may
it be to make thee, at least, as wise a man as thy father.

LADY WRONGHEAD.

Miss Jenny, don't you see your cousin, child?   450

MANLY.

And for thee, my pretty dear (*salutes her*), mayst thou
be, at least, as good a woman as thy mother.

JENNY.

I wish I may ever be so handsome, sir.

MANLY.

Ha, Miss Pert!— (*Aside.*) Now that's a thought that
seems to have been hatched in the girl on this side 455
Highgate.

SIR FRANCIS.

Her tongue is a little nimble, sir.

LADY WRONGHEAD.

That's only from her country education, Sir Francis. You
know she has been kept too long there. —So I brought
her to London, sir, to learn a little more reserve and 460
modesty.

MANLY.

Oh, the best place in the world for it; every woman she
meets will teach her something of it. There's the good
gentlewoman of the house, looks like a knowing person;
even she perhaps will be so good as to show her a little 465
London behavior.

MRS. MOTHERLY.

Alas, sir, Miss won't stand long in need of my instructions.

---

450. *cousin*] loosely used, until the mid-eighteenth century, to refer
to any relative.

456. *Highgate*] at that time a village some four miles from London,
standing on one of the main routes to the north.

MANLY (*aside*).

> That I dare say. What thou canst teach her, she will
> soon be mistress of.   470

MRS. MOTHERLY.

> If she does, sir, they shall always be at her service.

LADY WRONGHEAD.

> Very obliging indeed, Mrs. Motherly.

SIR FRANCIS.

> Very kind, and civil, truly. —I think we are got into a
> mighty good hawse here.

MANLY.

> Oh yes, and very friendly company.   475

COUNT BASSET (*aside*).

> Humh! Egad I don't like his looks; he seems a little
> smoky. I believe I had as good brush off. If I stay, I
> don't know but he may ask me some odd questions.

MANLY.

> Well, sir, I believe you and I do but hinder the family—

COUNT BASSET.

> It's very true, sir, I was just thinking of going.— (*Aside*.) 480
> He don't care to leave me, I see. But it's no matter, we
> have time enough. —And so, ladies, without ceremony,
> your humble servant.

> > *Exit* Count Basset, *and drops a letter.*

LADY WRONGHEAD [*aside*].

> Ha, what paper's this? Some billet-doux, I'll lay my
> life—but this is no place to examine it.   485

> > *Puts it in her pocket.*

SIR FRANCIS.

> Why in such haste, cousin?

MANLY.

> Oh, my lady must have a great many affairs upon her
> hands, after such a journey.

LADY WRONGHEAD.

> I believe, sir, I shall not have much less every day,
> while I stay in this town, of one sort or other.   490

MANLY.

> Why truly, ladies seldom want employment here, madam.

---

477. *smoky*] suspicious, watchful.

JENNY.

And mamma did not come to it to be idle, sir.

MANLY.

Nor you neither I dare say, my young mistress.

JENNY.

I hope not, sir.

MANLY.

Hah, Miss Mettle! —Where are you going, sir?   495

SIR FRANCIS.

Only to see you to th' door, sir.

MANLY.

Oh Sir Francis, I love to come and go without ceremony.

SIR FRANCIS.

Nay sir, I must do as you will have me. Your humble
servant.   *Exit* Manly.

JENNY.

This cousin Manly, papa, seems to be but of an odd 500
sort of a crusty humor. I don't like him half so well as
the count.

SIR FRANCIS.

Pooh, that's another thing, child. Cousin is a little
proud indeed, but however you must always be civil
to him, for he has a deal of money—and nobody knows 505
who he may give it to.

LADY WRONGHEAD.

Pshah, a fig for his money! You have so many projects of
late about money, since you are a Parliament-man. What,
we must make ourselves slaves to his impertinent humors,
eight or ten years perhaps, in hopes to be his heirs—and 510
then he will be just old enough to marry his maid.

MRS. MOTHERLY.

Nay, for that matter, madam, the town says he is going
to be married already.

SIR FRANCIS.

Who, cousin Manly?

LADY WRONGHEAD.

To whom, pray?   515

---

509. *humors*] whims and fancies; moods.

MRS. MOTHERLY.

Why, is it possible your ladyship should know nothing of it? To my Lord Townly's sister, Lady Grace.

LADY WRONGHEAD.

Lady Grace!

MRS. MOTHERLY.

Dear madam, it has been in the newspapers.

LADY WRONGHEAD.

I don't like that neither.   520

SIR FRANCIS.

Naw I do, for then it's likely it mayn't be true.

LADY WRONGHEAD (*aside*).

If it is not too far gone, at least it may be worth one's while to throw a rub in his way.

SQUIRE RICHARD.

Pray feyther, haw lung will it be to supper?

SIR FRANCIS.

Odso, that's true. Step to the cook, lad, and ask what she 525 can get us.

MRS. MOTHERLY.

If you please, sir, I'll order one of my maids to show her where she may have anything you have a mind to.

SIR FRANCIS.

Thank you kindly, Mrs. Motherly.   [*Exit* Mrs. Motherly.]

SQUIRE RICHARD.

Od's flesh! What, is not it i' th' hawse yet? I shall be 530 famished. But howld—I'll go and ask Doll an' there's none o' th' goose poy left.

SIR FRANCIS.

Do so, and dost hear, Dick?—see if there's e'er a bottle o' th' strung beer that came i' th' coach with us. If there be, clap a toast in it, and bring it up.   535

SQUIRE RICHARD.

With a little nutmeg, and sugar, shawn't I, feyther?

SIR FRANCIS.

Aye, aye, as thee and I always drink it for breakfast. Go thy ways—and I'll fill a pipe i' th' meanwhile.

---

535. *a toast*] a piece of toasted bread placed in beer or wine.

Takes one from a pocket-case, and fills it.
Exit Squire Richard.

LADY WRONGHEAD.

This boy is always thinking of his belly.

SIR FRANCIS.

Why my dear, you may allow him to be a little hungry 540
after his journey.

LADY WRONGHEAD.

Nay, even breed him your own way. He has been cram-
ming, in or out of the coach, all this day I am sure. I
wish my poor girl could eat a quarter as much.

JENNY.

Oh for that, I could eat a great deal more, mamma; but 545
then mayhap I should grow coarse, like him, and spoil
my shape.

LADY WRONGHEAD.

Aye, so thou wouldst, my dear.

Enter Squire Richard *with a full tankard.*

SQUIRE RICHARD.

Here, feyther, I ha' browght it. It's well I went as I
did, for our Doll had just baked a toast, and was going 550
to drink it herself.

SIR FRANCIS.

Why then, here's to thee, Dick.   *Drinks.*

SQUIRE RICHARD.

Thonk yow, feyther.

LADY WRONGHEAD.

Lord, Sir Francis. I wonder you can encourage the boy to
swill so much of that lubberly liquor. It's enough to 555
make him quite stupid.

SQUIRE RICHARD.

Why it niver hurts me, mother, and I sleep like a hawnd
after it.   *Drinks.*

SIR FRANCIS.

I am sure I ha' drunk it these thirty years; and by your
leave, madam, I don't know that I want wit. Ha ha! 560

---

549. *as*] when (dialect).
555. *lubberly*] vulgar and stupefying.

JENNY.

But you might have had a great deal more, papa, if you
would have been governed by my mother.

SIR FRANCIS.

Daughter, he that is governed by his wife has no wit at
all.

JENNY.

Then I hope I shall marry a fool, sir, for I love to 565
govern dearly.

SIR FRANCIS.

You are too pert, child. It don't do well in a young
woman.

LADY WRONGHEAD.

Pray Sir Francis, don't snub her. She has a fine growing
spirit, and if you check her so you will make her as dull 570
as her brother there.

SQUIRE RICHARD (after a long draught).

Indeed mother, I think my sister is too forward.

JENNY.

You! You think I'm too forward, sure, brother mud!
Your head's too heavy to think of anything but your
belly.   575

LADY WRONGHEAD.

Well said, miss. He's none of your master, though he is
your elder brother.

SQUIRE RICHARD.

No, nor she shawn't be my mistress, while she's younger
sister.

SIR FRANCIS.

Well said, Dick. Show 'em that stawt liquor makes a 580
stawt heart, lad.

SQUIRE RICHARD.

So I wull, and I'll drink ageen, for all her.   *Drinks.*

Enter John Moody.

SIR FRANCIS.

So John, how are the horses?

---

582. *for all her*] in spite of all she says.

JOHN MOODY.

Troth sir, I ha' noa good opinion o' this tawn; it's
made up o' mischief, I think.   585

SIR FRANCIS.

What's the matter, naw?

JOHN MOODY.

Why, I'st tell your worship. Before we were gotten to
th' street end with the coach here, a great lugger-headed
cart, with wheels as thick as a brick wall, laid hawl'd
on't, and has poo'd it aw to bits. Crack! went the perch, 590
down goes the coach, and whang! says the glasses, all to
shivers. Marcy upon us! And this be London, would we
were aw weell i' th' country ageen.

JENNY.

What have you to do, to wish us all in the country again,
Mr. Lubber? I hope we shall not go into the country 595
again these seven years, mamma, let twenty coaches be
pulled to pieces.

SIR FRANCIS.

Hold your tongue, Jenny. —Was Roger in no fault in all
this?

JOHN MOODY.

Noa, sir, nor I, noather. "Are not yow asheamed," says 600
Roger to the carter, "to do such an unkind thing by
strangers?" "Noa," says he, "you bumkin." Sir, he did
the thing on very purpose, and so the folks said that
stood by. "Very well," says Roger, "yow shall see what

587. I'st] *01–2*; I'll *03*.

---

587. *I'st*] I'll; see textual note, and note to *we'st ta'*, l. 265 above.
588. *lugger-headed*] a pseudo-dialect variant of *logger-headed*, "thick-
headed, stupid," hence "clumsy."
589. *wheels . . . wall*] The wheels of London carts were noted for
their solidity and thickness.
590. *poo'd*] pulled, i.e., shattered.
590. *perch*] "The long or main timber of a carriage, which unites
the hind and fore ends together" (William Felton, *A Treatise on
Carriage* [London, 1794–1795], II, 229).
591. *glasses*] coach windows.
596. *seven years*] By the Septennial Act of 1716 the life of a Parliament was fixed at seven years.

our meyster will say to ye!" "Your meyster?" says he;   605
"your meyster may kiss my ——," and so he clapped his
hand just there, and like your worship. Flesh, I thowght
they had better breeding in this tawn.

SIR FRANCIS.

I'll teach this rascal some, I warrant him. Od's bud, if
I take him in hand I'll play the devil with him.   610

SQUIRE RICHARD.

Aye do, feyther, have him before the Parliament.

SIR FRANCIS.

Od's bud, and so I will. I will make him know who I am.
Where does he live?

JOHN MOODY.

I believe—in London, sir.

SIR FRANCIS.

What's the rascal's name?   615

JOHN MOODY.

I think I heard somebody call him Dick.

SQUIRE RICHARD.

What, my name?

SIR FRANCIS.

Where did he go?

JOHN MOODY.

Sir, he went home.

SIR FRANCIS.

Where's that?   620

JOHN MOODY.

By my troth, sir, I doan't know. I heard him say he would
cross the same street again tomorrow, and if we had a
mind to stand in his way, he would pooll us over and
over again.

SIR FRANCIS.

Will he so! Od's zooks, get me a constable.   625

---

613. *Where does he live*] Sir Francis and his servants are unaware
that all London carts were officially registered, and compelled by law
to display their registration number so that complaints could be
lodged against their drivers.

625. *Od's zooks*] "by God's hooks" (the nails of the Cross).

LADY WRONGHEAD.

Pooh, get you a good supper. Come, Sir Francis, don't
put yourself in a heat for what can't be helped. Accidents
will happen to people that travel abroad to see the
world. For my part, I think it's a mercy it was not
overturned before we were all out on't.   630

SIR FRANCIS.

Why aye, that's true again, my dear.

LADY WRONGHEAD.

Therefore see tomorrow if we can buy one at second
hand, for present use; so bespeak a new one, and then
all's easy.

JOHN MOODY.

Why troth, sir, I doan't think this could have held you 635
above a day longer.

SIR FRANCIS.

D'ye think so, John?

JOHN MOODY.

Why you ha' had it ever sen' your worship were high
sheriff.

SIR FRANCIS.

Why then, go and see what Doll has got us for supper, 640
and come and get off my boots.

Exit Sir Francis [*and* John Moody].

LADY WRONGHEAD.

In the meantime, Miss, do you step to Handy, and bid
her get me some fresh night-clothes.   *Exit* Lady Wronghead.

JENNY.

Yes, mamma, and some for myself too.   *Exit* Jenny.

SQUIRE RICHARD.

Od's flesh, and what mun I do all alone?   645
I'll e'en seek out where t'other pratty miss is.
And she and I'll go plays at cards for kisses.   *Exit.*

---

643. *night-clothes*] clothes for informal evening wear (see Mrs.
Delany, vol. II, p. 6).

ACT III

Scene: the Lord Townly's house.
Enter Lord Townly, *a* Servant *attending.*

LORD TOWNLY.

Who's there?

SERVANT.

My lord!

LORD TOWNLY.

Bid them get dinner. [*Exit* Servant.]

Enter Lady Grace.

Lady Grace, your servant.

LADY GRACE.

What, is the house up already? My lady is not dressed   5
yet.

LORD TOWNLY.

No matter, it's three o'clock. She may break my rest, but
she shall not alter my hours.

LADY GRACE.

Nay, you need not fear that now, for she dines abroad.

LORD TOWNLY.

That, I suppose, is only an excuse for her not being   10
ready yet.

LADY GRACE.

No, upon my word, she is engaged to company.

LORD TOWNLY.

Where, pray?

LADY GRACE.

At my Lady Revel's; and you know they never dine till
supper-time.   15

LORD TOWNLY.

No, truly; she is one of those orderly ladies who never
let the sun shine upon any of their vices. But prithee,
sister, what humor is she in today?

LADY GRACE.

Oh, in tip-top spirits, I can assure you. She won a good
deal last night.   20

---

7. *three o'clock*] the customary hour for dinner.

LORD TOWNLY.

I know no difference between her winning or losing,
while she continues her course of life.

LADY GRACE.

However, she is better in good humor than bad.

LORD TOWNLY.

Much alike. When she is in good humor, other people
only are the better for it; when in a very ill humor—then, 25
indeed, I seldom fail to have my share of her.

LADY GRACE.

Well, we won't talk of that now. Does anybody dine
here?

LORD TOWNLY.

Manly promised me—by the way, madam, what do you
think of his last conversation?   30

LADY GRACE [*pausing*].

I am a little at a stand about it.

LORD TOWNLY.

How so?

LADY GRACE.

Why—I don't know how he can ever have any thoughts
of me, that could lay down such severe rules upon wives
in my hearing.   35

LORD TOWNLY.

Did you think his rules unreasonable?

LADY GRACE.

I can't say I did. But he might have had a little more
complaisance before me, at least.

LORD TOWNLY.

Complaisance is only a proof of good breeding, but his
plainness was a certain proof of his honesty, nay, of his   40
good opinion of you. For he would never have opened
himself so freely, but in confidence that your good sense
could not be disobliged at it.

LADY GRACE.

My good opinion of him, brother, has hitherto been
guided by yours. But I have received a letter this morn-   45
ing that shows him a very different man from what I
thought him.

LORD TOWNLY.

A letter! From whom?

LADY GRACE.

That I don't know, but there it is.   *Gives a letter.*

LORD TOWNLY.

Pray let's see.   *Reads.* 50
    "The enclosed, madam, fell accidentally into my
    hands. If it no way concerns you, you will only
    have the trouble of reading this, from your sincere
    friend and humble servant,

                                      Unknown, etc."   55

LADY GRACE.

And this was the enclosed.   *Giving another.*

LORD TOWNLY (*reads*).

    "To Charles Manly, Esq.,
    Your manner of living with me of late, convinces me
    that I now grow as painful to you as to myself; but
    however, though you can love me no longer, I hope you   60
    will not let me live worse than I did, before I left an
    honest income for the vain hopes of being ever yours.
                                      Myrtilla Dupe

    P.S. 'Tis above four months since I received a shilling
    from you."   65

LADY GRACE.

What think you now?

LORD TOWNLY.

I am considering—

LADY GRACE.

You see it's directed to him—

LORD TOWNLY.

That's true; but the postscript seems to be a reproach
that I think he is not capable of deserving.   70

LADY GRACE.

But who could have concern enough to send it to me?

LORD TOWNLY.

I have observed that these sort of letters from unknown
friends—generally come from secret enemies.

LADY GRACE.

What would you have me do in it?

LORD TOWNLY.

What I think you ought to do: fairly show it him, and 75
say I advised you to it.

LADY GRACE.

Will not that have a very odd look, from me?

LORD TOWNLY.

Not at all, if you use my name in it. If he is innocent,
his impatience to appear so will discover his regard to
you. If he is guilty, it will be your best way of preventing 80
his addresses.

LADY GRACE.

But what pretense have I to put him out of countenance?

LORD TOWNLY.

I can't think there's any fear of that.

LADY GRACE.

Pray what is't you do think then?

LORD TOWNLY.

Why, certainly that it's much more probable this letter 85
may be all an artifice, than that he is in the least concerned in it.

Enter a Servant.

SERVANT.

Mr. Manly, my lord. [*Exit* Servant.]

LORD TOWNLY.

Do you receive him, while I step a minute in to my lady.

Exit Lord Townly.

Enter Manly.

MANLY.

Madam, your most obedient. They told me my lord 90
was here.

LADY GRACE.

He will be here presently; he is but just gone in to my
sister.

MANLY.

So! Then my lady dines with us?

---

82. *pretense*] right, justification.

LADY GRACE.

No, she is engaged.   95

MANLY.

I hope you are not of her party, madam?

LADY GRACE.

Not till after dinner.

MANLY.

And pray how may she have disposed of the rest of the day?

LADY GRACE.

Much as usual. She has visits till about eight; after that, 100
till court-time, she is to be at quadrille, at Mrs. Idle's;
after the Drawing-room she takes a short supper with
my Lady Moonlight, and from thence they go together
to my Lord Noble's assembly.

MANLY.

And are you to do all this with her, madam?   105

LADY GRACE.

Only a few of the visits. I would indeed have drawn her
to the play, but I doubt we have so much upon our
hands, *that* will not be practicable.

MANLY.

But how can you forbear all the rest of it?

LADY GRACE.

There's no great merit in forbearing what one is not 110
charmed with.

MANLY.

And yet I have found that very difficult, in my time.

LADY GRACE.

How do you mean?

MANLY.

Why, I have passed a great deal of my life in the hurry
of the ladies, though I was generally better pleased when 115
I was at quiet without 'em.

---

101. *court-time*] "Court hour . . . is half an hour after nine" (Mrs.
Delany, vol. I, p. 178).

102. *Drawing-room*] On two or three evenings a week the king and
queen received visitors in the great drawing room, or audience chamber, at St. James's Palace. The visitors might well stay until 11
P.M. or later.

LADY GRACE.

What induced you, then, to be with them?

MANLY.

Idleness, and the fashion.

LADY GRACE.

No mistresses in the case?

MANLY.

To speak honestly—yes. Being often in the toyshop, 120
there was no forbearing the baubles.

LADY GRACE.

And of course, I suppose, sometimes you were tempted to
pay for them twice as much as they were worth.

MANLY.

Why really, where fancy only makes the choice, madam,
no wonder if we are generally bubbled in those sort of 125
bargains—which I confess has been often my case. For I
had constantly some coquette or other upon my hands,
whom I could love perhaps just enough to put it in her
power to plague me.

LADY GRACE.

And that's a power, I doubt, commonly made use of.   130

MANLY.

The amours of a coquette, madam, seldom have any other
view. I look upon them, and prudes, to be nuisances just
alike, though they seem very different. The first are
always plaguing the men, and the other are always abus-
ing the women.   135

LADY GRACE.

And yet both of them do it for the same vain ends, to
establish a false character of being virtuous.

MANLY.

Of being chaste, they mean, for they know no other
virtue; and upon the credit of that, they traffic in everything else that's vicious. They (even against Nature) 140
keep their chastity, only because they find they have more
power to do mischief with it than they could possibly
put in practice without it.

---

120. *toyshop*] fancy goods shop, selling snuffboxes, fans, watches, etc.
125. *bubbled*] cheated.

LADY GRACE.

Hold, Mr. Manly. I am afraid this severe opinion of the
sex is owing to the ill choice you have made of your 145
mistresses.

MANLY.

In a great measure, it may be so. But, madam, if both
these characters are so odious, how vastly valuable is
that woman who has attained all they aim at, without the
aid of the folly or vice of either?   150

LADY GRACE.

I believe those sort of women to be as scarce, sir, as the
men that believe there are any such; or that allowing
such, have virtue enough to deserve them.

MANLY.

That *could* deserve them then—had been a more favorable reflection.   155

LADY GRACE.

Nay, I speak only from my little experience. For I'll
be free with you, Mr. Manly: I don't know a man in the
world that, in appearance, might better pretend to a
woman of the first merit, than yourself; and yet I have
a reason, in my hand here, to think you have your 160
failings.

MANLY.

I have infinite, madam; but I am sure the want of an
implicit respect for you is not among the number. Pray
what is in your hand, madam?

LADY GRACE.

Nay, sir, I have no title to it, for the direction is to 165
you.   *Gives him a letter.*

MANLY.

To me! I don't remember the hand—   *Reads to himself.*

LADY GRACE (*aside*).

I can't perceive any change of guilt in him, and his surprise seems natural. —Give me leave to tell you one
thing by the way, Mr. Manly: that I should never have 170
shown you this but that my brother enjoined me to it.

MANLY.

I take that to proceed from my lord's good opinion of
me, madam.

LADY GRACE.

I hope, at least, it will stand as an excuse for my taking
this liberty.   175

MANLY.

I never yet saw you do anything, madam, that wanted an
excuse; and I hope you will not give me an instance to
the contrary by refusing the favor I am going to ask
you.

LADY GRACE.

I don't believe I shall refuse any that you think proper   180
to ask.

MANLY.

Only this, madam: to indulge me so far as to let me
know how this letter came into your hands.

LADY GRACE.

Enclosed to me in this, without a name.

MANLY.

If there be no secret in the contents, madam—   185

LADY GRACE.

Why—there is an impertinent insinuation in it; but as I
know your good sense will think it so too, I will venture
to trust you.

MANLY.

You oblige me, madam.

> *He takes the other letter, and reads.*

LADY GRACE (*aside*).

Now am I in the oddest situation! Methinks our conver-   190
sation grows terribly critical. This must produce something. Oh lud, would it were over!

MANLY.

Now, madam, I begin to have some light into the poor
project that is at the bottom of all this.

LADY GRACE.

I have no notion of what could be proposed by it.   195

MANLY.

A little patience, madam. First, as to the insinuation you
mention—

LADY GRACE (*aside*).

Oh, what is he going to say now?

MANLY.

> Though my intimacy with my lord may have allowed my
> visits to have been very frequent here of late, yet in 200
> such a talking town as this you must not wonder if a
> great many of those visits are placed to your account.
> And this taken for granted, I suppose has been told to
> my Lady Wronghead as a piece of news, since her arrival,
> not improbably without many more imaginary circum- 205
> stances.

LADY GRACE.

> My Lady Wronghead!

MANLY.

> Aye madam, for I am positive this is her hand.

LADY GRACE.

> What view could she have in writing it?

MANLY.

> To interrupt any treaty of marriage she may have heard 210
> I am engaged in; because if I die without heirs her
> family expects that some part of my estate may return
> to them again. But (I hope) she is so far mistaken, that
> if this letter has given you the least uneasiness—I shall
> think that the happiest moment of my life.   215

LADY GRACE.

> That does not carry your usual complaisance, Mr. Manly.

MANLY.

> Yes madam, because I am sure I can convince you of my
> innocence.

LADY GRACE.

> I am sure I have no right to inquire into it.

MANLY.

> Suppose you may not, madam; yet you may very inno- 220
> cently have so much curiosity.

LADY GRACE (aside).

> With what an artful gentleness he steals into my opin-
> ion! —Well sir, I won't pretend to have so little of the
> woman in me as to want curiosity. But pray, do you
> suppose then this "Myrtilla" is a real or a fictitious name? 225

---

205. *not improbably without*] very probably with.

MANLY.

Now I recollect, madam, there is a young woman in the
house where my Lady Wronghead lodges, that I heard
somebody call Myrtilla. This letter may be written by
her—but how it came directed to me, I confess is a
mystery that, before I ever presume to see your ladyship 230
again, I think myself obliged in honor to find out.   *Going.*

LADY GRACE.

Mr. Manly, you are not going?

MANLY.

'Tis but to the next street, madam; I shall be back in
ten minutes.

LADY GRACE.

Nay, but dinner's just coming up.   235

MANLY.

Madam, I can neither eat nor rest till I see an end of
this affair.

LADY GRACE.

But this is so odd. Why should any silly curiosity of
mine drive you away?

MANLY.

Since you won't suffer it to be yours, madam, then it 240
shall be only to satisfy my own curiosity.   *Exit* Manly.

LADY GRACE.

Well—and now, what am I to think of all this? Or
suppose an indifferent person had heard every word we
have said to one another, what would *they* have thought
on't? Would it have been very absurd to conclude, he is 245
seriously inclined to pass the rest of his life with me?
I hope not—for I am sure the case is terribly clear on
my side. And why may not I, without vanity, suppose
my unaccountable somewhat has done as much execution upon him? Why, because he never told me so. Nay, 250
he has not so much as mentioned the word love, or ever
said one civil thing to my person. Well, but he has said
a thousand to my good opinion, and has certainly got it.

---

249. *unaccountable somewhat*] inexplicable charm. This phrase, and
others like it (e.g., "the unexpressible somewhat") were quite orthodox
ways of rendering the French phrase *je ne sais quoi.* Cf. *Provoked
Wife,* IV.ii.64.

Had he spoke first to my person, he had paid a very ill
compliment to my understanding. I should have thought 255
him impertinent, and never have troubled my head
about him. But as he has managed the matter, at least
I am sure of one thing: that let his thoughts be what they
will, I shall never trouble my head about any other man
as long as I live.   260

Enter Mrs. Trusty.

Well, Mrs. Trusty, is my sister dressed yet?

TRUSTY.

Yes, madam; but my lord has been courting her so, I
think, till they are both out of humor.

LADY GRACE.

How so?

TRUSTY.

Why, it begun, madam, with his lordship's desiring her 265
ladyship to dine at home today—upon which my lady said
she could not be ready. Upon that, my lord ordered them
to stay the dinner, and then my lady ordered the coach.
Then my lord took her short, and said he had ordered
the coachman to set up. Then my lady made him a great 270
curtsy, and said she would wait till his lordship's horses
had dined, and was mighty pleasant. But for fear of the
worst, madam, she whispered me—to get her chair ready.

Exit Mrs. Trusty.

LADY GRACE.

Oh, here they come; and by their looks seem a little unfit
for company.   *Exit* Lady Grace. 275

Enter Lady Townly, Lord Townly *following.*

LADY TOWNLY.

Well, look you, my lord: I can bear it no longer! Nothing
still but about my faults, my faults! An agreeable subject
truly.

LORD TOWNLY.

Why, madam, if you won't hear of them, how can I
ever hope to see you mend them?   280

---

270. *to set up*] to stable and feed the horses.

LADY TOWNLY.

Why, I don't intend to mend them. I can't mend them.
You know I have tried to do it an hundred times, and—
it hurts me so, I can't bear it!

LORD TOWNLY.

And I, madam, can't bear this daily licentious abuse of
your time and character.   285

LADY TOWNLY.

Abuse? Astonishing! —when the universe knows I am
never better company than when I am doing what I have
a mind to. But to see this world, that men can never
get over that silly spirit of contradiction! Why, but last
Thursday now—there you wisely amended one of my 290
faults, as you call them; you insisted upon my not going
to the masquerade—and pray, what was the consequence?
Was not I as cross as the devil all the night after? Was
not I forced to get company at home, and was not it
almost three o'clock in the morning before I was able 295
to come to myself again? And then the fault is not
mended neither, for next time I shall only have twice
the inclination to go. So that all this mending and mending, you see, is but darning an old ruffle—to make it
worse than it was before.   300

LORD TOWNLY.

Well, the manner of women's living, of late, is insupportable; and one way or other—

LADY TOWNLY.

It's to be mended, I suppose! Why, so it may. But then,
my dear lord, you must give one time—and when things
are at worst, you know, they may mend themselves. 305
Ha, ha!

LORD TOWNLY.

Madam, I am not in a humor, now, to trifle.

LADY TOWNLY.

Why then, my lord, one word of fair argument; to talk
with you your own way now. You complain of my late

290. amended] *03*; mended *01-2*.

304-305. *when things . . . themselves*] a neat modification of the
proverb "When things are at the worst they will mend."

hours, and I of your early ones. So far are we even, 310
you'll allow. But pray, which gives us the best figure
in the eye of the polite world—my active, spirited three
in the morning, or your dull, drowsy eleven at night?
Now, I think *one* has the air of a woman of quality,
and t'*other* of a plodding mechanic, that goes to bed 315
betimes that he may rise early to open his shop—faugh!

LORD TOWNLY.

Fie, fie, madam, is this your way of reasoning? 'Tis
time to wake you then. 'Tis not your ill hours alone
that disturb me, but as often the ill company that occasion those ill hours.   320

LADY TOWNLY.

Sure I don't understand you now, my lord; what ill company do I keep?

LORD TOWNLY.

Why, at best, women that lose their money, and men that
win it. Or, perhaps, men that are voluntary bubbles at
one game, in hopes a lady will give them fair play at 325
another. Then that unavoidable mixture with known
rakes, concealed thieves, and sharpers in embroidery—or
what to me is still more shocking, that herd of familiar
chattering crop-eared coxcombs, who are so often like
monkeys there would be no knowing them asunder but 330
that their tails hang from their head, and the monkey's
grows where it should do.

LADY TOWNLY.

And a husband must give eminent proof of his sense, that
thinks their powder-puffs dangerous.

---

315. *mechanic*] often used contemptuously for any manual worker
or tradesman.

324. *bubbles*] dupes.

329. *crop-eared*] with their hair cut short at the sides, leaving the
ears conspicuous.

331. *tails*] The hair on men's wigs was usually gathered at the
nape of the neck so that it hung down the back either in two "ties"
or in a single plaited "queue" which was often encased in a ribbon.
Beaus were increasingly preferring the queue-wig to the tie-wig.

334. *powder-puffs*] Fops used an instrument like a small bellows
to powder their wigs and coats.

LORD TOWNLY.
Their being fools, madam, is not always the husband's 335
security. Or if it were, Fortune sometimes gives them
advantages might make a thinking woman tremble.

LADY TOWNLY.
What do you mean?

LORD TOWNLY.
That women, sometimes, lose more than they are able to
pay; and if a creditor be a little pressing the lady may be 340
reduced to try if, instead of gold, the gentleman will
accept of a trinket.

LADY TOWNLY.
My lord, you grow scurrilous. You'll make me hate you.
I'll have you to know I keep company with the politest
people in town, and the assemblies I frequent are full 345
of such.

LORD TOWNLY.
So are the churches—now and then.

LADY TOWNLY.
My friends frequent them too, as well as the assemblies.

LORD TOWNLY.
Yes, and would do it oftener—if a groom of the chambers
there were allowed to furnish cards to the company.   350

LADY TOWNLY.
I see what you drive at all this while. You would lay an
imputation on my fame, to cover your own avarice. I
might take any pleasures, I find, that were not expensive.

LORD TOWNLY.
Have a care, madam. Don't let me think you only value
your chastity to make me reproachable for not indulging 355
you in everything else that's vicious. I, madam, have a
reputation too to guard, that's dear to me as yours. The
follies of an ungoverned wife may make the wisest man
uneasy; but 'tis his own fault if ever they make him
contemptible.   360

LADY TOWNLY.
My lord, you would make a woman mad!

---

349. *groom of the chambers*] the principal footman in a noble household.

LORD TOWNLY.

You'd make a man a fool.

LADY TOWNLY.

If heaven has made you otherwise, that won't be in my power.

LORD TOWNLY.

Whatever may be in your inclination, madam, I'll pre- 365 vent your making me a beggar, at least.

LADY TOWNLY.

A beggar? Croesus! I'm out of patience. I won't come home till four tomorrow morning.

LORD TOWNLY.

That may be, madam; but I'll order the doors to be locked at twelve.   370

LADY TOWNLY.

Then I won't come home till tomorrow night.

LORD TOWNLY.

Then, madam—you shall never come home again.

Exit Lord Townly.

LADY TOWNLY.

What does he mean? I never heard such a word from him in my life before; the man always used to have manners, in his worst humors. There's something that I don't 375 see, at the bottom of all this. But his head's always upon some impracticable scheme or other, so I won't trouble mine any longer about him.

Enter Manly.

Mr. Manly, your servant.

MANLY.

I ask pardon for my intrusion, madam; but I hope my 380 business with my lord will excuse it.

LADY TOWNLY.

I believe you'll find him in the next room, sir.

MANLY.

Will you give me leave, madam?

---

367. *Croesus*] the last and richest king of Lydia (ca. 550 B.C.), and a byword for wealth.

LADY TOWNLY.

Sir, you have my leave, though you were a lady.

MANLY (*aside*).

What a well-bred age do we live in!   *Exit* Manly. 385

Enter Lady Grace.

LADY TOWNLY.

Oh my dear Lady Grace, how could you leave me so
unmercifully alone all this while?

LADY GRACE.

I thought my lord had been with you.

LADY TOWNLY.

Why yes, and therefore I wanted your relief, for he has
been in such a fluster here—   390

LADY GRACE.

Bless me, for what?

LADY TOWNLY.

Only our usual breakfast. We have each of us had our
dish of matrimonial comfort this morning; we have been
charming company.

LADY GRACE.

I am mighty glad of it. Sure it must be a vast happiness 395
when a man and a wife can give themselves the same
turn of conversation.

LADY TOWNLY.

Oh, the prettiest thing in the world.

LADY GRACE.

Now I should be afraid that where two people are every
day together so, they must often be in want of some- 400
thing to talk upon.

LADY TOWNLY.

Oh my dear, you are the most mistaken in the world.
Married people have things to talk of, child, that never
enter into the imagination of others. Why, here's my lord
and I now, we have not been married above two short 405
years, you know, and we have already eight or ten things
constantly in bank, that whenever we want company we
can take up any one of them for two hours together, and
the subject never the flatter. Nay, if we have occasion

for it, it will be as fresh next day too as it was the first 410
hour it entertained us.

LADY GRACE.

Certainly, that must be vastly pretty.

LADY TOWNLY.

Oh, there's no life like it! Why t'other day for example,
when you dined abroad, my lord and I, after a pretty
cheerful *tête-à-tête* meal, sat us down by the fireside in 415
an easy, indolent, pick-tooth way, for about a quarter
of an hour, as if we had not thought of one another's
being in the room. At last, stretching himself and yawn-
ing, "My dear," says he, "aw—you came home very late,
last night." " 'Twas but just turned of two," says I. "I 420
was abed—aw—by eleven," says he. "So you are every
night," says I. "Well," says he, "I am amazed you can
sit up so late." "How can you be amazed," says I, "at
a thing that happens so often?" Upon which we entered
into a conversation; and though this is a point has 425
entertained us above fifty times already, we always find
so many pretty, new things to say upon it that I believe,
in my soul, it will last as long as we live.

LADY GRACE.

But pray, in such sort of family dialogues (though
extremely well for passing the time) don't there, now 430
and then, enter some little witty sort of bitterness?

LADY TOWNLY.

Oh yes, which does not do amiss at all. A smart repartee,
with a zest of recrimination at the head of it, makes the
prettiest sherbet. Aye, aye, if we did not mix a little
of the acid with it, a matrimonial society would be so 435
luscious that nothing but an old lickerish prude would
be able to bear it.

LADY GRACE.

Well, certainly you have the most elegant taste—

LADY TOWNLY.

Though to tell you the truth, my dear, I rather think we
squeezed a little too much lemon into it, this bout. For 440
it grew so sour at last that—I think—I almost told him

---

433. *zest*] orange or lemon peel, used as a piquant flavoring.

he was a fool, and he, again—talked something oddly of—
turning me out of doors!

LADY GRACE.

Oh, have a care of that!

LADY TOWNLY.

Nay, if he should, I may thank my own wise father for 445
that—

LADY GRACE.

How so?

LADY TOWNLY.

Why, when my good lord first opened his honorable
trenches before me, my unaccountable papa, in whose
hands I then was, gave me up at discretion.   450

LADY GRACE.

How do you mean?

LADY TOWNLY.

He said the wives of this age were come to that pass that
he would not desire even his own daughter should be
trusted with pin money; so that my whole train of separate inclinations are left entirely at the mercy of an 455
husband's odd humors.

LADY GRACE.

Why that, indeed, is enough to make a woman of spirit
look about her.

LADY TOWNLY.

Nay, but to be serious, my dear: what would you really
have a woman do in my case?   460

LADY GRACE.

Why, if I had as sober a husband as you have, I would
make myself the happiest wife in the world—by being
as sober as he.

LADY TOWNLY.

Oh, you wicked thing, how can you tease one at this rate
—when you know he is so very sober that (except giving 465
me money) there is not one thing in the world he can do
to please me? And I at the same time, partly by nature,

---

450. *at discretion*] unconditionally, without making terms—a military
phrase, completing the image of siege-warfare.

454. *pin money*] an allowance settled on a wife at marriage, for her
personal expenses.

and partly perhaps by keeping the best company, do
with my soul love almost everything he hates. I dote
upon assemblies; my heart bounds at a ball; and at an 470
opera—I expire! Then I love play, to distraction. Cards
enchant me, and dice—put me out of my little wits. Dear,
dear hazard! Oh, what a flow of spirits it gives one! Do
you never play at hazard, child?

LADY GRACE.

Oh, never. I don't think it sits well upon women; there's 475
something so masculine, so much the air of a rake in it.
You see how it makes the men swear and curse, and
when a woman is thrown into the same passion, why—

LADY TOWNLY.

That's very true. One is a little put to it, sometimes,
not to make use of the same words to express it.   480

LADY GRACE.

Well, and upon ill luck, pray what words are you really
forced to make use of?

LADY TOWNLY.

Why, upon a very hard case, indeed, when a sad wrong
word is rising just to one's tongue's end, I give a great
gulp—and swallow it.   485

LADY GRACE.

Well, and is not that enough to make you forswear play
as long as you live?

LADY TOWNLY.

Oh yes, I have forsworn it.

LADY GRACE.

Seriously?

LADY TOWNLY.

Solemnly, a thousand times; but then one is constantly 490
forsworn.

LADY GRACE.

And how can you answer that?

LADY TOWNLY.

My dear, what we say when we are losers we look upon
to be no more binding than a lover's oath, or a great
man's promise. But I beg pardon, child; I should not 495
lead you so far into the world. You are a prude, and
design to live soberly.

LADY GRACE.

Why, I confess my nature and my education do, in a
good degree, incline me that way.

LADY TOWNLY.

Well, how a woman of spirit (for you don't want that, 500
child) can dream of living soberly, is to me inconceivable.
For you will marry, I suppose?

LADY GRACE.

I can't tell but I may.

LADY TOWNLY.

And won't you live in town?

LADY GRACE.

Half the year, I should like it very well.   505

LADY TOWNLY.

My stars! and you would really live in London half the
year, to be sober in it?

LADY GRACE.

Why not?

LADY TOWNLY.

Why can't you as well go and be sober in the country?

LADY GRACE.

So I would—t'other half year.   510

LADY TOWNLY.

And pray, what comfortable scheme of life would you
form now, for your summer and winter sober entertainments?

LADY GRACE.

A scheme that I think might very well content us.

LADY TOWNLY.

Oh, of all things let's hear it.   515

LADY GRACE.

Why, in summer I could pass my leisure hours in riding,
in reading, walking by a canal, or sitting at the end of

516–517. in riding, in reading] *03*;
in riding—soberly! in reading *01*;
in riding, reading *02*.

---

517. *canal*] a long, narrow, rectangular lake—a form of garden ornament that was going out of fashion.

it under a great tree; in dressing, dining, chatting with
an agreeable friend, perhaps hearing a little music,
taking a dish of tea, or a game at cards, soberly; man- 520
aging my family, looking into its accounts, playing with
my children (if I had any), or in a thousand other innocent amusements—soberly! And possibly, by these means,
I might induce my husband to be as sober as myself.

LADY TOWNLY.

Well my dear, thou art an astonishing creature; for sure 525
such primitive antediluvian notions of life have not been
in any head these thousand years. Under a great tree,
o' my soul! But I beg we may have the sober town-
scheme too, for I am charmed with the country one.

LADY GRACE.

You shall, and I'll try to stick to my sobriety there too. 530

LADY TOWNLY.

Well, though I am sure it will give me the vapors, I
must hear it however.

LADY GRACE.

Why then, for fear of your fainting, madam, I will first
so far come into the fashion that I would never be
dressed out of it—but still it should be soberly; for I 535
can't think it any disgrace to a woman of my private
fortune, not to wear her lace as fine as the wedding suit
of a first duchess. Though there is one extravagance I
would venture to come up to—

LADY TOWNLY.

Aye, now for it—   540

LADY GRACE.

I would every day be as clean as a bride.

LADY TOWNLY.

Why, the men say that's a great step to be made one.
Well now you are dressed; pray let's see to what purpose.

518. tree] *03*; tree—soberly *01–2*.

---

531. *vapors*] a collective name for a number of nervous disorders,
including giddiness, depression, and irritability, supposedly caused by
vapors ascending to the brain; a fashionable ailment among upper-
class women.

LADY GRACE.

I would visit—that is, my real friends; but as little for
form as possible. I would go to court, sometimes to an 545
assembly, nay play at quadrille—soberly. I would see
all the good plays, and (because 'tis the fashion) now
and then an opera; but I would not expire there, for fear
I should never go again. And lastly: I can't say, but for
curiosity, if I liked my company, I might be drawn in 550
once to a masquerade. And this, I think, is as far as
any woman can go—soberly.

LADY TOWNLY.

Well, if it had not been for that last piece of sobriety,
I was just going to call for some surfeit-water.

LADY GRACE.

Why, don't you think, with the farther aid of break- 555
fasting, dining, taking the air, supping, sleeping, not
to say a word of devotion, the four-and-twenty hours
might roll over in a tolerable manner?

LADY TOWNLY.

Tolerable? Deplorable! Why, child, all you propose is
but to *endure* life; now I want to *enjoy* it.   560

Enter Mrs. Trusty.

MRS. TRUSTY.

Madam, your ladyship's chair is ready.

LADY TOWNLY.

Have the footmen their white flambeaux yet?—for last
night I was poisoned.

MRS. TRUSTY.

Yes madam, there were some come in this morning.

Exit Trusty.

LADY TOWNLY.

My dear, you will excuse me; but you know my time is 565
so precious—

544. visit] *03*; visit—soberly *01–2*.   548. but I] *03*; but still soberly;
                                            I *01*; but *02*.

554. *surfeit-water*] a medicine for sickness and indigestion, distilled
from poppies and herbs.
562. *white flambeaux*] wax torches, as opposed to the inferior kind
made of wicks dipped in pitch.

LADY GRACE.

That I beg I may not hinder your least enjoyment of it.

LADY TOWNLY.

You will call me at Lady Revel's?

LADY GRACE.

Certainly.

LADY TOWNLY.

But I am so afraid it will break into your scheme, my 570
dear.

LADY GRACE.

When it does, I will—soberly break from you.

LADY TOWNLY.

Why then, till we meet again, dear sister, I wish you all
tolerable happiness.   *Exit* Lady Townly.

LADY GRACE.

There she goes—dash! into her stream of pleasures. Poor 575
woman, she is really a fine creature, and sometimes infinitely agreeable. Nay, take her out of the madness of
this town, rational in her notions and easy to live with.
But she is so borne down by this torrent of vanity
in vogue, she thinks every hour of her life is lost that 580
she does not lead at the head of it. What it will end
in, I tremble to imagine. —Ha, my brother, and Manly
with him. I guess what they have been talking of. I
shall hear it in my turn, I suppose, but it won't become
me to be inquisitive.   *Exit* Lady Grace. 585

Enter Lord Townly *and* Manly.

LORD TOWNLY.

I did not think my Lady Wronghead had such a notable
brain—though I can't say she was so very wise in trust-
ing this silly girl you call Myrtilla with the secret.

MANLY.

No my lord, you mistake me. Had the girl been in the
secret, perhaps I had never come at it myself.   590

LORD TOWNLY.

Why, I thought you said the girl writ this letter to you,
and that my Lady Wronghead sent it enclosed to my
sister?

MANLY.

If you please to give me leave, my lord, the fact is thus:
this enclosed letter to Lady Grace was a real original one, 595
written by this girl to the count we have been talking
of. The count drops it, and my Lady Wronghead finds
it. Then only changing the cover, she seals it up as a
letter of business, just written by herself to me; and pre-
tending to be in a hurry, gets this innocent girl to write 600
the direction for her.

LORD TOWNLY.

Oh, then the girl did not know she was superscribing
a billet-doux of her own, to you?

MANLY.

No, my lord; for when I first questioned her about the
direction she owned it immediately. But when I showed 605
her that her letter to the count was within it, and told
her how it came into my hands, the poor creature was
amazed, and thought herself betrayed both by the count
and my lady. In short, upon this discovery the girl and
I grew so gracious that she has let me into some trans- 610
actions in my Lady Wronghead's family which, with my
having a careful eye over them, may prevent the ruin
of it.

LORD TOWNLY.

You are very generous to be so solicitous for a lady that
has given you so much uneasiness.   615

MANLY.

But I will be most unmercifully revenged of her, for I
will do her the greatest friendship in the world—against
her will.

LORD TOWNLY.

What an uncommon philosophy art thou master of, to
make even thy malice a virtue!   620

MANLY.

Yet, my lord, I assure you there is no one action of my
life gives me more pleasure than your approbation of it.

---

602. *superscribing*] writing the address (or *direction*, l. 601) on the
cover of the letter.

610. *gracious*] friendly, well disposed to one another.

LORD TOWNLY.

Dear Charles! my heart's impatient till thou art nearer
to me. And as a proof that I have long wished thee so—
while your daily conduct has chosen rather to deserve, 625
than ask, my sister's favor, I have been as secretly indus-
trious to make her sensible of your merit. And since on
this occasion you have opened your whole heart to me,
'tis now with equal pleasure I assure you we have both
succeeded. She is as firmly yours—   630

MANLY.

Impossible, you flatter me!

LORD TOWNLY.

I'm glad you think it flattery; but she herself shall prove
it none. She dines with us alone. When the servants are
withdrawn, I'll open a conversation that shall excuse my
leaving you together. Oh Charles, had I, like thee, been 635
cautious in my choice, what melancholy hours had this
heart avoided!

MANLY.

No more of that, I beg, my lord—

LORD TOWNLY.

But 'twill at least be some relief to my anxiety (however
barren of content the state has been to me) to see so 640
near a friend and sister happy in it. Your harmony of
life will be an instance how much the choice of temper
is preferable to beauty.

    While your soft hours in mutual kindness move,
    You'll reach by virtue what I lost by love.   *Exeunt.* 645

642–643. temper is] *03*; temper's
01–2.

---

640. *state*] of matrimony.

ACT IV

MRS. MOTHERLY.

So, niece! Where is it possible you can have been these six hours?

MYRTILLA.

Oh madam, I have such a terrible story to tell you!

MRS. MOTHERLY.

A story, od's my life! What have you done with the count's note of five hundred pound I sent you about? 5
Is it safe? It is good? Is it security?

MYRTILLA.

Yes, yes, it is safe. But for its goodness—mercy on us, I have been in a fair way to be hanged about it!

MRS. MOTHERLY.

The dickens! Has this rogue of a count played us another trick then? 10

MYRTILLA.

You shall hear, madam. When I came to Mr. Cash the banker's and showed him his note for five hundred pounds, payable to the count, or order, in two months, he looked earnestly upon it and desired me to step into the inner room while he examined his books. After I 15
had stayed about ten minutes he came in to me, claps to the door, and charges me with a constable for forgery.

MRS. MOTHERLY.

Ah, poor soul, and how didst thou get off?

MYRTILLA.

While I was ready to sink in this condition, I begged him to have a little patience till I could send for Mr. 20
Manly, whom he knew to be a gentleman of worth and honor, and who I was sure would convince him, whatever fraud might be in the note, that I was myself an innocent, abused woman. And as good luck would have it, in less than half an hour Mr. Manly came. So, without 25

---

8. *hanged*] because it was a capital offense to forge a bank note or bank bill.

mincing the matter, I fairly told him upon what design the count had lodged that note in your hands, and in short laid open the whole scheme he had drawn us into to make our fortune.

MRS. MOTHERLY.

The devil you did! 30

MYRTILLA.

Why how do you think it was possible I could any otherways make Mr. Manly my friend, to help me out of the scrape I was in? To conclude, he soon made Mr. Cash easy and sent away the constable; nay farther promised me, if I would trust the note in his hands he would 35 take care it should be fully paid before it was due, and at the same time would give me an ample revenge upon the count. So that all you have to consider now, madam, is whether you think yourself safer in the count's hands, or Mr. Manly's. 40

MRS. MOTHERLY.

Nay, nay, child, there is no choice in the matter. Mr. Manly may be a friend indeed, if anything in our power can make him so.

MYRTILLA.

Well, madam, and now pray how stand matters at home here? What has the count done with the ladies? 45

MRS. MOTHERLY.

Why everything he has a mind to do, by this time, I suppose. He is in as high favor with Miss as he is with my lady.

MYRTILLA.

Pray, where are the ladies?

MRS. MOTHERLY.

Rattling abroad in their own coach, and the well-bred 50 count along with them. They have been scouring all the shops in town over, buying fine things and new clothes, from morning to night. They have made one voyage already, and have brought home such a cargo of baubles and trumpery—mercy on the poor man that's to pay for 55 them!

MYRTILLA.

Did not the young squire go with them?

MRS. MOTHERLY.

No, no. Miss said, truly he would but disgrace their
party, so they even left him asleep by the kitchen fire.

MYRTILLA.

Has not he asked after me all this while? For I had a   60
sort of an assignation with him.

MRS. MOTHERLY.

Oh yes, he has been in a bitter taking about it. At last
his disappointment grew so uneasy that he fairly fell
a-crying; so to quiet him I sent one of the maids and
John Moody abroad with him, to show him—the lions,   65
and the Monument. Od's me, there he is, just come home
again. You may have business with him, so I'll even turn
you together.   [*Exit* Mrs. Motherly.]

Enter Squire Richard.

SQUIRE RICHARD.

Soah, soah, Mrs. Myrtilla, wheere han yow been aw this
day, forsooth?   70

MYRTILLA.

Nay, if you go to that, squire, where have you been,
pray?

SQUIRE RICHARD.

Why, when I fun' 'at yow were no loikely to come
whoam, I were ready to hong mysel'. So John Moody,
and I, and one o' your lasses have been—Lord knows   75
where—a-seeing o' soights.

66. there] *03*; here *01–2*.   68.1. *Enter* Squire Richard] *01,*
67. turn] *02–3*; leave *01*.   *03*; *Exit* Myrtilla *02, which omits*
                                         the whole of the ensuing dia-
                                         logue, lines 69–159.

62. *taking*] passion, state of agitation.
65–66. *the lions, and the Monument*] the two most famous sights
of London. The King's menagerie was housed in the Tower. The
Monument, designed by Wren, is a stone column commemorating the
Great Fire. A spiral staircase (345 steps) inside the column leads to
an open balcony with extensive views over the City.
70. *forsooth*] madam (see note to II.213).

MYRTILLA.

Well, and pray what have you seen, sir?

SQUIRE RICHARD.

Flesh, I cawn't tell, not I—seen everything, I think.
First there we went o' top o' the what-d'ye-call-it there,
the great huge stone post, up the rawnd and rawnd   80
stairs that twine and twine about, just an' as thof it
were a corkscrew.

MYRTILLA.

Oh, the Monument! Well, and was not it a fine sight,
from the top of it?

SQUIRE RICHARD.

Sight, miss? I know no'—I saw nowght but smoke and   85
brick housen, and steeple tops. Then there was such a
mortal ting-tang of bells, and rumbling of carts and
coaches, and then the folks under one looked so small,
and made such a hum and a buzz, it put me in mind of
my mother's great glass beehive, in our garden in the   90
country.

MYRTILLA.

I think, master, you give a very good account of it.

SQUIRE RICHARD.

Aye, but I did no' like it; for my head, my head, begun
to turn—so I trundled me dawn stairs agen, like a round
trencher.   95

MYRTILLA.

Well, but this was not all you saw, I suppose?

SQUIRE RICHARD.

Noa, noa, we went after that and saw the lions, and I
liked them better by hawlf; they are pure grim devils.
Hoh, hoh! I touke a stick, and gave one of them such a
poke o' the noase—I believe he would ha' snapped my   100
head off, an' he could ha' got me. Hoh, hoh, hoh!

MYRTILLA.

Well, master, when you and I go abroad I'll show you
prettier sights than these. There's a masquerade tomorrow.

---

86. *housen*] houses (a dialect plural form).

SQUIRE RICHARD.

Oh laud, aye, they say that's a pure thing for Merry- 105
Andrews, and those sort of comical mummers. And the
count tells me that there lads and lasses may jig their
tails, and eat, and drink, without grudging, all night
lung.

MYRTILLA.

What would you say now, if I should get you a ticket, 110
and go along with you?

SQUIRE RICHARD.

Ah dear!

MYRTILLA.

But have a care, squire, the fine ladies there are terribly
tempting. Look well to your heart, or ad's me! they'll
whip it up in the trip of a minute.   115

SQUIRE RICHARD.

Aye, but they cawn't thoa; soa let 'um look to themselves. An' ony of 'um falls in love with me—mayhap they
had as good be quiet.

MYRTILLA.

Why sure you would not refuse a fine lady, would you?

SQUIRE RICHARD.

Aye, but I would though, unless it were—one 'at I know 120
of.

MYRTILLA.

Oh ho, then you have left your heart in the country, I
find?

SQUIRE RICHARD.

Noa, noa, my heart—eh—my heart een't awt o' this room.

MYRTILLA.

I am glad you have it about you, however.   125

105–106. *Merry-Andrews*] professional clowns or buffoons who performed at fairs. Such clowns often wore the lozenge-patterned harle-
quin costume which was much in favor at masquerades.

106. *mummers*] actors in a rustic *mumming*, a Christmas and New
Year entertainment in which men and women exchanged clothes and
went about the village singing and dancing.

108. *without grudging*] to their hearts' content.

SQUIRE RICHARD.

> Nay, mayhap not soa noather. Somebody else may have it,
> 'at you little think of.

MYRTILLA.

> I can't imagine what you mean.

SQUIRE RICHARD.

> Noa? Why, doan't yow know how many folks there is in
> this room, naw?   130

MYRTILLA.

> Very fine, master, I see you have learned the town gal-
> lantry already.

SQUIRE RICHARD.

> Why, doan't you believe 'at I have a kindness for you,
> then?

MYRTILLA.

> Fie, fie, master, how you talk! Beside you are too young 135
> to think of a wife.

SQUIRE RICHARD.

> Aye, but I caun't help thinking o' yow, for all that.

MYRTILLA.

> How! Why sure, sir, you don't pretend to think of me in
> a dishonorable way?

SQUIRE RICHARD.

> Nay, that's as yow see good. I did no' think 'at yow 140
> would ha' thowght of me for a husband, mayhap, unless
> I had means in my own hands; and feyther allows me
> but hawlf-a-crown a week, as yet awhile.

MYRTILLA.

> Oh, when I like anybody, 'tis not want of money will
> make me refuse them.   145

SQUIRE RICHARD.

> Well, that's just my mind now; for an' I like a girl,
> miss, I would take her in her smuck.

---

147. *smuck*] smock. "The usual expression when a gallant agreed to
take a bride without a dowry was 'take her in her smock' . . ."
(*The Works of John Dryden*, ed. H. T. Swedenberg et al., vol. VIII
[Berkeley and Los Angeles, 1962], p. 261; note to *The Wild Gallant,*
V.v.69).

MYRTILLA.

Aye, master, now you speak like a man of honor. This
shows something of a true heart in you.

SQUIRE RICHARD.

Aye, and a true heart you'll find me; try when you will. 150

MYRTILLA.

Hush, hush, here's your papa come home, and my aunt
with him.

SQUIRE RICHARD.

A devil rive 'em, what do they come naw for?

MYRTILLA.

When you and I get to the masquerade, you shall see
what I'll say to you.   155

SQUIRE RICHARD.

Well, hands upon't then—

MYRTILLA.

There—

SQUIRE RICHARD.

One buss, and a bargain. (*Kisses her.*) Ad's wauntlikins, as soft and plump as a marrow-pudding.

Exeunt severally.

Enter Sir Francis Wronghead *and* Mrs. Motherly.

SIR FRANCIS.

What, my wife and daughter abroad, say you?   160

MRS. MOTHERLY.

Oh dear sir, they have been mighty busy all the day long.
They just came home to snap up a short dinner, and
so went out again.

SIR FRANCIS.

Well, well, I shan't stay supper for 'em, I can tell 'em
that. For od's heart, I have had nothing in me but a 165
toast and tankard, since morning.

159.1. *and* Mrs. Motherly] *01, 03*;   160. say you] *01, 03*; Mrs. Moth-
om. *02.*   erly *02.*

---

153. *rive 'em*] tear them in pieces.
158. *One buss . . . bargain*] perhaps proverbial. Cf. "Buss (*or* kiss)
and be friends."
159. *marrow-pudding*] a succulent country delicacy made from bread
soaked in milk, minced marrow, eggs, sugar, nutmeg, and almonds.

MRS. MOTHERLY.

I am afraid, sir, these late parliament hours won't agree with you.

SIR FRANCIS.

Why, truly, Mrs. Motherly, they don't do right with us country gentlemen. To lose one meal out of three is a 170 hard tax upon a good stomach.

MRS. MOTHERLY.

It is so indeed, sir.

SIR FRANCIS.

But hawsomever, Mrs. Motherly, when we consider that what we suffer is for the good of our country—

MRS. MOTHERLY.

Why truly, sir, that is something.   175

SIR FRANCIS.

Oh, there's a great deal to be said for't. The good of one's country is above all things. A true-hearted Englishman thinks nothing too much for it. I have heard of some honest gentlemen so very zealous that for the good of their country—they would sometimes go to dinner at 180 midnight.

MRS. MOTHERLY.

Oh, the goodness of 'em! Sure their country must have a vast esteem for them!

SIR FRANCIS.

So they have, Mrs. Motherly. They are so respected when they come home to their boroughs, after a session, and 185 so beloved—that their country will come and dine with them every day in the week.

MRS. MOTHERLY.

Dear me, what a fine thing 'tis to be so populous.

SIR FRANCIS.

It is a great comfort indeed, and I can assure you, you are a good sensible woman, Mrs. Motherly.   190

MRS. MOTHERLY.

Oh dear sir, your honor's pleased to compliment.

SIR FRANCIS.

No, no, I see you know how to value people of consequence.

MRS. MOTHERLY.

Good lack, here's company, sir. Will you give me leave
to get you a broiled bone, or so, till the ladies come 195
home, sir?

SIR FRANCIS.

Why troth, I don't think it would be amiss.

MRS. MOTHERLY.

It shall be done in a moment, sir.   *Exit.*

Enter Manly.

MANLY.

Sir Francis, your servant.

SIR FRANCIS.

Cousin Manly!   200

MANLY.

I am come to see how the family goes on here.

SIR FRANCIS.

Troth, all as busy as bees. I have been upon the wing
ever since eight o'clock this morning.

MANLY.

By your early hour, then, I suppose you have been making your court to some of the great men.   205

SIR FRANCIS.

Why, faith, you have hit it, sir. I was advised to lose
no time, so I e'en went straight forward, to one great
man I had never seen in my life before.

MANLY.

Right, that was doing business. But who had you got to
introduce you?   210

SIR FRANCIS.

Why, nobody. I remembered I had heard a wise man say,
"My son, be bold"—so, troth, I introduced myself.

195. a broiled bone, or so] *01–2;*
a little something *03.*

211–212. *wise man . . . be bold*] The "wise man" here may simply
be Sir Francis's father. On the other hand the "wise man said" formula
was often jocularly used to introduce a piece of conventional wisdom.
A number of proverbs enjoin boldness, though not precisely in these
words, as also does Ecclesiasticus 19:10.

MANLY.

As how, pray?

SIR FRANCIS.

Why thus, look ye. "Please your lordship," says I, "I am
Sir Francis Wronghead of Bumper Hall, and Member of 215
Parliament for the Borough of Guzzledown." "Sir, your
humble servant," says my lord. "Thof I have not the
honor to know your person, I have heard you are a very
honest gentleman, and I am glad your borough has made
choice of so worthy a representative. And so," says he, 220
"Sir Francis, have you any service to command me?"
Naw, cousin, those last words, you may be sure, gave
me no small encouragement. And thof I know, sir, you
have no extraordinary opinion of my parts, yet I believe
you won't say I missed it naw.   225

MANLY.

Well, I hope I shall have no cause.

SIR FRANCIS.

So, when I found him so courteous—"My lord," says I,
"I did not think to ha' troubled your lordship with
business upon my first visit; but since your lordship is
pleased not to stand upon ceremony—why truly," says I, 230
"I think naw is as good as another time."

MANLY.

Right, there you pushed him home.

SIR FRANCIS.

Aye, aye, I had a mind to let him see that I was none of
your mealy-mouthed ones.

MANLY.

Very good.   235

SIR FRANCIS.

"So in short, my lord," says I, "I have a good estate, but—
a—it's a leetle awt at elbows; and as I desire to serve my
King, as well as my country, I shall be very willing to
accept of a place at court."

---

232. *pushed him home*] pressed him hard, thrust to the heart of
the matter.

239. *place*] a profitable position at court. There were at this time
at least thirty "places," some of them sinecures, which were worth
£1,000 a year (approximately £15,000 in modern terms) or more.

MANLY.

So, this was making short work on't.   240

SIR FRANCIS.

Ecod, I shot him flying, cousin. Some of your hawlf-witted ones naw, would ha' hummed and hawed, and dangled a month or two after him, before they durst open their mouths about a place, and, mayhap, not ha' got it at last neither.   245

MANLY.

Oh, I'm glad you're so sure on't—

SIR FRANCIS.

You shall hear, cousin. "Sir Francis," says my lord, "pray what sort of a place may you ha' turned your thowghts upon?" "My lord," says I, "beggars must not be choosers. But ony place," says I, "about a thousand 250 a year, will be well enough to be doing with till something better falls in"—for I thowght it would not look well to stond haggling with him at first.

MANLY.

No, no, your business was to get footing any way.

SIR FRANCIS.

Right, there's it! Ah cousin, I see you know the world. 255

MANLY.

Yes, yes, one sees more of it every day. Well, but what said my lord to all this?

SIR FRANCIS.

"Sir Francis," says he, "I shall be glad to serve you any way that lies in my power." So he gave me a squeeze by the hond, as much as to say, "Give yourself no trouble, 260 I'll do your business." With that he turned him abawt to somebody with a colored ribbon across here, that looked, in my thowghts, as if he came for a place too.

MANLY.

Ha! So, upon these hopes you are to make your fortune!

SIR FRANCIS.

Why, do you think there's ony doubt of it, sir?   265

248. a] *03*; *om. 01–2*.

241. *Ecod*] a variant of "egad." Members of the Orders of Knighthood wore a broad sash-like ribbon diagonally across the breast.
262. *With a colored . . . here*] Members of the Orders.

MANLY.

Oh no, I have not the least doubt about it—for just as
you have done, I made my fortune ten years ago.

SIR FRANCIS.

Why, I never knew you had a place, cousin.

MANLY.

Nor I neither, upon my faith, cousin. But you perhaps
may have better fortune; for I suppose my lord has heard 270
of what importance you were in the debate today. You
have been since down at the House, I presume?

SIR FRANCIS.

Oh yes. I would not neglect the House, for ever so much.

MANLY.

Well, and pray what have they done there?

SIR FRANCIS.

Why, troth, I can't well tell you what they have done, but 275
I can tell you what I did—and I think pretty well in the
main. Only I happened to make a little mistake at
last, indeed.

MANLY.

How was that?

SIR FRANCIS.

Why, they were all got there into a sort of a puzzling 280
debate about the Good of the Nation—and I were always
for that, you know. But in short, the arguments were so
long-winded o' both sides that—waunds, I did no' well
understand 'um. Hawsomever, I was convinced, and so
resolved to vote right, according to my conscience. So, 285
when they came to put the question, as they call it, I
don't know haw 'twas—but I doubt I cried "Aye" when I
should ha' cried "No."

MANLY.

How came that about?

SIR FRANCIS.

Why, by a mistake, as I tell you. For there was a good- 290
humored sort of a gentleman (one Mr. Totherside I

284. I was] 03; I I was 01–2.

---

281. *Good of the Nation*] a political catch phrase.
286. *put the question*] put the matter to the vote.

think they call him) that sat next me, as soon as I had
cried "Aye" gives me a hearty shake by the hand. "Sir,"
says he, "you are a man of honor and a true Englishman,
and I should be proud to be better acquainted with 295
you." And so with that, he takes me by the sleeve, along
with the crowd, into the lobby. So, I knew nowght—but
od's flesh, I was got o' th' wrung side the post. For I
were told afterwards, I should have stayed where I was.

MANLY.
And so, if you had not quite made your fortune before, 300
you have clinched it now.— (*Aside.*) Ah, thou head of the
Wrongheads!

SIR FRANCIS.
Odso, here's my lady come home at last. I hope, cousin,
you will be so kind as to take a family supper with us?

MANLY.
Another time, Sir Francis; but tonight I am engaged. 305

Enter Lady Wronghead, Miss Jenny, *and* Count Basset.

LADY WRONGHEAD.
Cousin, your servant. I hope you will pardon my rude-
ness, but we have really been in such a continual hurry
here that we have not had a leisure moment to return
your last visit.

MANLY.
Oh madam, I am a man of no ceremony. You see *that* 310
has not hindered my coming again.

LADY WRONGHEAD.
You are infinitely obliging; but I'll redeem my credit
with you.

293. Aye] *03*; No *01–2*.

292–299. *as soon as . . . where I was*] The first vote on a measure
was by word of mouth, the Members shouting "Aye" or "Nay." If
this vote was indecisive it was usual for the "Ayes" to withdraw into
an outer lobby or hall, and to be counted as they filed back into the
Chamber. The "Nays" were counted as they sat. Sir Francis has
unluckily voted against the Government, presumably on a censure
motion by the Opposition.

MANLY.

 At your own time, madam.

COUNT BASSET.

 I must say that for Mr. Manly, madam; if making people 315
easy is the rule of good breeding, he is certainly the
best-bred man in the world.

MANLY (*aside*).

 Soh! I am not to drop my acquaintance, I find. —I am
afraid, sir, I shall grow vain upon your good opinion.

COUNT BASSET.

 I don't know that, sir. But I am sure, what you are 320
pleased to say makes me so.

MANLY (*aside*).

 The most impudent modesty that ever I met with.

LADY WRONGHEAD (*aside*).

 Lard, how ready his wit is!

SIR FRANCIS (*apart*).

 Don't you think, sir, the count's a very fine gentleman?

MANLY.

 Oh, among the ladies, certainly.   325

SIR FRANCIS.

 And yet he's as stout as a lion. Waund, he'll storm anything.

MANLY.

 Will he so? Why then, sir, take care of your citadel.

SIR FRANCIS.

 Ah, you are a wag, cousin.

MANLY.

 I hope, ladies, the town air continues to agree with you? 330

JENNY.

 Oh, perfectly well, sir. We have been abroad in our new
coach all day long, and we have bought an ocean of fine
things. And tomorrow we go to the masquerade, and
on Friday to the play, and on Saturday to the opera,
and on Sunday we are to be at the what-d'ye-call-it— 335
assembly, and see the ladies play at quadrille, and piquet,

---

318. *Soh*] an exclamation of scorn, irritation, and distaste.
336. *piquet*] a card game for two players, fashionable among women.

and ombre, and hazard, and basset. And on Monday we
are to see the King! And so on Tuesday—

LADY WRONGHEAD.

Hold, hold, miss; you must not let your tongue run so
fast, child. You forget! You know I brought you hither 340
to learn modesty.

MANLY (aside).

Yes, yes, and she is improved with a vengeance.

JENNY.

Lawrd, mamma, I am sure I did not say any harm. And if
one must not speak in one's turn, one may be kept under
as long as one lives, for aught I see.   345

LADY WRONGHEAD.

O' my conscience, this girl grows so headstrong—

SIR FRANCIS.

Aye, aye, there's your fine growing spirit for you! Now
tack it dawn, an' you can.

JENNY.

All I said, papa, was only to entertain my cousin Manly.

MANLY.

My pretty dear, I am mightily obliged to you.   350

JENNY.

Look you there now, madam.

LADY WRONGHEAD.

Hold your tongue, I say.

JENNY (turning away and glouting).

I declare it, I won't bear it.— (Aside to the Count.) She
is always a-snubbing me before you, sir. I know why she
does it, well enough—   355

COUNT BASSET (aside [to Jenny]).

Hush, hush, my dear, don't be uneasy at that. She'll
suspect us.

337–338. *Monday . . . the King*] The royal Drawing-room held on
Monday evening was usually the most crowded of the week. Members
of the gentry and *bourgeoisie* found it relatively easy to gain admittance on that day.

348. *tack it dawn*] take it down; i.e., subdue it.

353. S.D. *glouting*] pouting, looking sullen.

JENNY.

Let her suspect, what do I care? I don't know but I have
as much reason to suspect as she, though perhaps I'm not
so 'fraid of her.   360

COUNT BASSET (*aside*).

Egad, if I don't keep a tight hand on my tit here, she'll
run away with my project before I can bring it to bear.

LADY WRONGHEAD (*aside*).

Perpetually hanging upon him! The young harlot is
certainly in love with him; but I must not let them see
I think so. And yet I can't bear it. —Upon my life, 365
Count, you'll spoil that forward girl. You should not
encourage her so.

COUNT BASSET.

Pardon me, madam, I was only advising her to observe
what your ladyship said to her.

MANLY (*aside*).

Yes truly, her observations have been something par- 370
ticular.

COUNT BASSET (*apart*).

In one word, madam, she has a jealousy of your ladyship, and I am forced to encourage her, to blind it. 'Twill
be better to take no notice of her behavior to me.

LADY WRONGHEAD.

You are right. I will be more cautious.   375

COUNT BASSET.

Tomorrow at the masquerade we may lose her.

LADY WRONGHEAD.

We shall be observed. I'll send you a note and settle
that affair. Go on with the girl, and don't mind me.

COUNT BASSET [*to* Jenny].

I have been taking your part, my little angel.

LADY WRONGHEAD.

Jenny, come hither child. You must not be so hasty, my 380
dear. I only advise you for your good.

---

361. *tit*] a small horse; like "jade" the word was often applied scorn-
fully to young women.
370–371. *something particular*] somewhat personal and pointed.

JENNY.

Yes, mamma; but when I am told of a thing before
company, it always makes me worse, you know.

MANLY (*aside*).

If I have any skill in the fair sex, Miss and her mamma
have only quarrelled because they are both of a mind. 385
This facetious count seems to have made a very genteel
step into the family.

Enter Myrtilla. Manly *talks apart with her.*

LADY WRONGHEAD.

Well, Sir Francis, and what news have you brought us
from Westminster today?

SIR FRANCIS.

News, madam? Ecod, I have some—and such as does not 390
come every day, I can tell you. A word in your ear: I
have got a promise of a place at court of a thousand
pawnd a year, already.

LADY WRONGHEAD.

Have you so, sir? And pray who may you thank for it?
Now who's in the right? Is not this better than throw- 395
ing so much away after a stinking pack of fox-hounds
in the country? Now your family may be the better
for it.

SIR FRANCIS.

Nay, that's what persuaded me to come up, my dove.

LADY WRONGHEAD.

Mighty well. Come, let me have another hundred pound 400
then.

SIR FRANCIS.

Another, child? Waunds, you have had one hundred this
morning; pray what's become of that, my dear?

LADY WRONGHEAD.

What's become of it? Why I'll show you, my love. Jenny,
have you the bills about you? 405

JENNY.

Yes, mamma.

---

386. *facetious*] urbane, smooth.
399. *come up*] travel up to London.

LADY WRONGHEAD.

> What's become of it? Why, laid out, my dear, with fifty
> more to it, that I was forced to borrow of the count here.

JENNY.

> Yes indeed, papa, and that would hardly do neither.
> There's th' account.   410

SIR FRANCIS *(turning over the bills)*.

> Let's see, let's see! What the devil have we got here?

MANLY *(apart [to Myrtilla])*.

> Then you have sounded your aunt, you say, and she
> readily comes in to all I proposed to you?

MYRTILLA.

> Sir, I'll answer with my life, she is most thankfully yours
> in every article. She mightily desires to see you, sir.   415

MANLY.

> I am going home directly. Bring her to my house in half
> an hour; and if she makes good what you tell me, you
> shall both find your account in it.

MYRTILLA.

> Sir, she shall not fail you.

SIR FRANCIS.

> Od's life, madam, here's nothing but toys, and trinkets, 420
> and fans, and clock-stockings, by wholesale!

LADY WRONGHEAD.

> There's nothing but what's proper, and for your credit,
> Sir Francis. Nay, you see I am so good a housewife that
> in necessaries for myself I have scarce laid out a shilling.

SIR FRANCIS.

> No, by my troth, so it seems; for the devil o' one thing's 425
> here that I can see you have any occasion for.

LADY WRONGHEAD.

> My dear, do you think I came hither to live out of the
> fashion? Why, the greatest distinction of a fine lady in
> this town is in the variety of pretty things that she has
> no occasion for.   430

---

420. *toys*] knickknacks.
421. *clock-stockings*] men's stockings patterned in gold or silver
thread; they were worn only by the finest of fine gentlemen.

JENNY.

Sure papa, could you imagine that women of quality
wanted nothing but stays and petticoats?

LADY WRONGHEAD.

Now that is so like him!

MANLY (*aside*).

So, the family comes on finely.

LADY WRONGHEAD.

Lard, if men were always to govern, what dowdies would   435
they reduce their wives to!

SIR FRANCIS.

An hundred pound in the morning, and want another
afore night! Waunds and fire, the Lord Mayor of London
could not hold it, at this rate.

MANLY (*aside*).

Oh, do you feel it, sir?   440

LADY WRONGHEAD.

My dear, you seem uneasy. Let me have the hundred
pound, and compose yourself.

SIR FRANCIS.

Compose the devil, madam! Why, do you consider what a
hundred pound a day comes to in a year?

LADY WRONGHEAD.

My life, if I account with you from one day to another,   445
that's really all that my head is able to bear at a time.
But I'll tell you what I consider; I consider that my
advice has got you a thousand pound a year this morning—*that* now, methinks, you might consider, sir.

SIR FRANCIS.

A thousand a year! Waunds, madam, but I have not   450
touched a penny of it yet.

MANLY (*aside*).

Nor never will, I'll answer for him.

Enter Squire Richard.

SQUIRE RICHARD.

Feyther, and yow doan't come quickly, the meat will be
coald; an' I'd fain pick a bit with you.

---

439. *hold it*] maintain such a style of life.

LADY WRONGHEAD.

Bless me, Sir Francis, you are not going to sup by 455
yourself?

SIR FRANCIS.

No, but I'm going to dine by myself, and that's pretty
near the matter, madam.

LADY WRONGHEAD.

Had not you as good stay a little, my dear? We shall
all eat in half an hour, and I was thinking to ask my 460
cousin Manly to take a family morsel with us.

SIR FRANCIS.

Nay, for my cousin's good company I don't care if I
ride a day's journey without baiting.

MANLY.

By no means, Sir Francis. I am going upon a little
business.   465

SIR FRANCIS.

Well sir, I know you don't love compliments.

MANLY.

You'll excuse me, madam—

LADY WRONGHEAD.

Since you have business, sir.   *Exit* Manly.

Enter Mrs. Motherly.

Oh, Mrs. Motherly, you were saying this morning you
had some very fine lace to show me; can't I see it now? 470
                                   Sir Francis *stares.*

MRS. MOTHERLY.

Why really, madam, I had made a sort of a promise to let
the Countess of Nicely have the first sight of it, for the
Birthday. But your ladyship—

LADY WRONGHEAD.

Oh, I die if I don't see it before her.

SQUIRE RICHARD (*apart*).

Woan't you goa, feyther?   475

457–458. *pretty near the matter*] pretty well what I intend to do.
463. *baiting*] stopping to take refreshment at an inn.
472–473. *the Birthday*] Receptions and balls were held at the Palace
to celebrate the royal birthdays; each guest would require ostenta-
tiously new and splendid clothes.

SIR FRANCIS.

Waunds, lad, I shall ha' noa stomach at this rate.

MRS. MOTHERLY.

Well madam, though I say it, 'tis the sweetest pattern
that ever came over; and for fineness, no cobweb comes
up to it.

SIR FRANCIS.

Od's guts and gizzard, madam, lace as fine as a cobweb? 480
Why what the devil's that to cost now?

MRS. MOTHERLY.

Nay, if Sir Francis does not like of it, madam—

LADY WRONGHEAD.

He like it! Dear Mrs. Motherly, he is not to wear it.

SIR FRANCIS.

Flesh, madam, but I suppose I am to pay for it.

LADY WRONGHEAD.

No doubt on't. Think of your thousand a year, and who 485
got it you. Go, eat your dinner and be thankful. Go.
(*Driving him to the door.*) Come Mrs. Motherly.

                    Exit Lady Wronghead, *with* Mrs. Motherly.

SIR FRANCIS.

Very fine! So here I mun fast, till I am almost famished
for the good of my country, while madam is laying me
out an hundred pound a day in lace as fine as a cobweb, 490
for the honor of my family! Od's flesh, things had need
go well, at this rate.

SQUIRE RICHARD.

Nay, nay, come feyther.

                    Exit Sir Francis [*with* Squire Richard].

Enter Mrs. Motherly.

MRS. MOTHERLY [*to* Jenny].

Madam, my lady desires you and the count will please to
come and assist her fancy in some of the new laces.   495

COUNT BASSET.

We'll wait upon her.   *Exit* Mrs. Motherly.

---

478. *came over*] i.e., from Flanders, where the finest and most expensive lace was made.

JENNY.

So, I told you how it was! You see she can't bear to
leave us together.

COUNT BASSET.

No matter, my dear. You know she has asked me to stay
supper. So, when your papa and she are abed, Mrs.   500
Myrtilla will let me into the house again; then may you
steal into her chamber, and we'll have a pretty sneaker
of punch together.

MYRTILLA.

Aye, aye, madam, you may command me anything.

JENNY.

Well, that will be pure!   505

COUNT BASSET.

But you had best go to her alone, my life. It will look
better if I come after you.

JENNY.

Aye, so it will. And tomorrow, you know, at the masquerade. And then, hey!

Sings.

Oh, I'll have a husband, aye marry,   510
   For why should I longer tarry
     Than other brisk girls have done?
For if I stay till I grow grey,
They'll call me old maid, and fusty old jade,
   So I'll no longer tarry,   515
   But I'll have a husband, aye marry,
     If money can buy me one.

501. may you] *01–2;* you may *03.*   510. aye] *03;* and *01–2. The first*
502. pretty] *03;* pretly *little 01–2.*   *line of the song is given at this*
                                         point in 01–3; 03 alone prints it
                                         in full, after the Epilogue.

---

502. *sneaker*] a small bowl.

505. *pure*] fine, splendid (see note on II.214).

509.1. *Sings*] The words and music for this song, and for the one
in V.iv, are by Henry Carey (ca. 1687–1743), composer, poet, and dramatist.

512. *brisk*] flirtatious, "fast."

My mother she says I'm too coming,
And still in my ears she is drumming
That I such vain thoughts should shun.   520
My sisters they cry "Oh fie and oh fie!"
But yet I can see, they're as coming as me.
So let me have husbands in plenty;
I'd rather have twenty times twenty
Than die an old maid undone.   525

Exit singing.

MYRTILLA.

So sir, am not I very commode to you?

COUNT BASSET.

Well child, and don't you find your account in it? Did
not I tell you we might still be of use to one another?

MYRTILLA.

Well, but how stands your affair with Miss, in the main?

COUNT BASSET.

Oh, she's mad for the masquerade! It drives like a nail; 530
we want nothing now but a parson, to clinch it. Did not
your aunt say she could get one at a short warning?

MYRTILLA.

Yes, yes, my Lord Townly's chaplain is her cousin you
know; he'll do your business and mine, at the same time.

COUNT BASSET.

Oh, it's true. But where shall we appoint him?   535

MYRTILLA.

Why you know my Lady Townly's house is always open
to the masks upon a ball-night, before they go to the
Haymarket.

COUNT BASSET.

Good.

MYRTILLA.

Now the doctor proposes we should all come thither in 540
our habits, and when the rooms are full we may steal

---

526. *commode*] accommodating, helpful—as a bawd or go-between
might be.
537–538. *masks . . . Haymarket*] After 1710 Vanbrugh's Theatre in
the Haymarket was used only for operas and (on Thursdays) for late
evening masquerades, euphemistically entitled "balls."
540. *doctor*] clergyman.
541. *habits*] masquerade costumes.

up into his chamber, he says, and there—crack! he'll give
us all a canonical commission to go to bed together.

COUNT BASSET.

Admirable. Well, the devil fetch me if I shall not be
heartily glad to see thee well settled, child.					545

MYRTILLA.

And may the black gentleman tuck me under his arm
at the same time, if I shall not think myself obliged to
you as long as I live.

COUNT BASSET.

One kiss, for old acquaintance sake. —Egad, I shall want
to be busy again!					550

MYRTILLA.

Oh you'll have one shortly that will find you employ-
ment. But I must run to my squire.

COUNT BASSET.

And I to the ladies. So your humble servant, sweet Mrs.
Wronghead.

MYRTILLA.

Yours, as in duty bound, most noble Count Basset.					555

Exit Myrtilla.

COUNT BASSET.

Why aye—Count! That title has been of some use to me
indeed. Not that I have any more pretense to it than I
have to a blue riband. Yet I have made a pretty considerable figure in life with it: I have lolled in my own
chariot, dealt at assemblies, dined with ambassadors, 560
and made one at quadrille with the first women of
quality. But—*tempora mutantur.* Since that damned

---

543. *canonical . . . together*] an echo of Etherege: "Please you, sir,
to commission a young couple to go to bed together a God's name"
(*The Man of Mode*, ed. W. B. Carnochan [Lincoln, Nebr., 1966],
V.ii.181–182).

558. *blue riband*] the badge of the Order of the Garter.

560. *dealt*] In the game of basset the dealer or banker had certain
privileges, as well as opportunities for sharp practice, so that the odds
were heavily weighted in his favor (Seymour, part I, p. 113).

562. *tempora mutantur*] The full form of this Anglo-Latin proverb
is *Tempora mutantur, et nos mutamur in illis:* "Times change, and we
change with them."

squadron at White's have left me out of their last secret,
I am reduced to trade upon my own stock of industry,
and make my last push upon a wife. If my card comes up 565
right (which I think can't fail) I shall once more cut
a figure, and cock my hat in the face of the best of them.
For since our modern men of fortune are grown wise
enough to be sharpers, I think sharpers are fools, that
don't take up the airs of men of quality.   *Exit.* 570

568. fortune] *03*; quality *01–2*.

___

563. *squadron*] organized gang of sharpers.

ACT V

[V. i] *Scene: Lord Townly's house.*
Enter Manly *and* Lady Grace.

MANLY.

There's something, madam, hangs upon your mind today;
is it unfit to trust me with it?

LADY GRACE.

Since you will know—my sister then—unhappy woman!—

MANLY.

What of her?

LADY GRACE.

I fear, is on the brink of ruin.   5

MANLY.

I am sorry for it. What has happened?

LADY GRACE.

Nothing so very *new*; but the continual repetition of it
at last has roused my brother to an intemperance that I
tremble at.

MANLY.

Have they had any words upon it?   10

LADY GRACE.

He has not seen her since yesterday.

MANLY.

What, not at home all night?

LADY GRACE.

About five this morning, in she came, but with such
looks, and such an equipage of misfortunes at her heels—
what can become of her?   15

MANLY.

Has not my lord seen her, say you?

LADY GRACE.

No, he changed his bed last night. I sat with him alone
till twelve in expectation of her; but when the clock
struck he started from his chair, and grew incensed to

2. is it . . . with it] *03*; *om. 01–2.*   3. know] *03*; know it *01–2.*
                                    8. roused] *01–2*; raised *03.*

_____

14. *equipage*] train, retinue.

− 120 −

that degree that had I not, almost on my knees, dis-   20
suaded him, he had ordered the doors, that instant,
to have been locked against her.

MANLY.

How terrible is his situation, when the most justifiable
severities he can use against her are liable to be the
mirth of all the dissolute card-tables in town!   25

LADY GRACE.

'Tis that, I know, has made him bear so long. But you,
that feel for him, Mr. Manly, will assist him to support
his honor, and if possible preserve his quiet. Therefore
I beg you don't leave the house till one or both of them
can be wrought to better temper.   30

MANLY.

How amiable is this concern, in you!

LADY GRACE.

For heaven's sake don't mind me, but think on something to preserve us all.

MANLY.

I shall not take the merit of obeying your commands,
madam, to serve my lord. But pray, madam, let me into   35
all that has passed since yesternight.

LADY GRACE.

When my entreaties had prevailed upon my lord, not to
make a story for the town by so public a violence as
shutting her at once out of his doors, he ordered the
next apartment to my lady's to be made ready for him.   40
While that was doing I tried, by all the little arts that
I was mistress of, to amuse him into temper; in short,
a silent grief was all I could reduce him to. On this,
we took our leaves, and parted to our repose. What
his was, I imagine by my own, for I ne'er closed my   45
eyes. About five, as I told you, I heard my lady at the
door; so I slipped on a gown, and sat almost an hour
with her in her own chamber.

MANLY.

What said she, when she did not find my lord there?

---

30. *temper*] state of mind, composure.

LADY GRACE.

Oh, so far from being shocked or alarmed at it, that she 50
blessed the occasion, and said that in her condition the
chat of a female friend was far preferable to the best
husband's company in the world.

MANLY.

Where has she spirits to support so much insensibility?

LADY GRACE.

Nay, 'tis incredible; for though she has lost every shil- 55
ling she had in the world, and stretched her credit
even to breaking, she rallied her own follies with such
vivacity, and painted the penance she knows she must
undergo for them in such ridiculous lights, that had not
my concern for a brother been too strong for her wit, 60
she had almost disarmed my anger.

MANLY.

Her mind may have another cast by this time. The most
flagrant dispositions have their hours of anguish, which
their pride conceals from company. But pray, madam,
how could she avoid coming down to dine? 65

LADY GRACE.

Oh, she took care of that before she went to bed, by
ordering her woman, whenever she was asked for, to say
she was not well.

MANLY.

You have seen her since she was up, I presume?

LADY GRACE.

Up? I question whether she be awake yet. 70

MANLY.

Terrible! What a figure does she make now! That Nature
should throw away so much beauty upon a creature, to
make such a slatternly use of it!

LADY GRACE.

O fie, there is not a more elegant beauty in town, when
she's dressed. 75

MANLY.

In my eye, madam, she that's early dressed has ten times
her elegance.

---

57. *rallied*] made fun of.

LADY GRACE.

But she won't be long now, I believe, for I think I see
her chocolate going up. —Mrs. Trusty, ahem!

       Mrs. Trusty *comes to the door.*

MANLY *(aside).*

Five o'clock in the afternoon, for a lady of quality's   80
breakfast, is an elegant hour indeed; which to show her
more polite way of living, too, I presume she eats in
her bed.

LADY GRACE *(to* Mrs. Trusty).

And when she is up, I would be glad she would let me
come to her toilet. That's all, Mrs. Trusty.   85

MRS. TRUSTY.

I will be sure to let her ladyship know, madam.

                         Exit Mrs. Trusty.

      Enter a Servant.

SERVANT.

Sir Francis Wronghead, sir, desires to speak with you.

MANLY.

He comes unseasonably. —What shall I do with him?

LADY GRACE.

Oh, see him by all means, we shall have time enough.
In the meanwhile I'll step in, and have an eye upon   90
my brother. Nay, nay, don't mind me, you have business.

MANLY.

You must be obeyed. *Retreating while* Lady Grace *goes out.*
Desire Sir Francis to walk in.   *Exit* Servant.
I suppose by this time his wise worship begins to find
that the balance of his journey to London is on the   95
wrong side.

      Enter Sir Francis.

Sir Francis, your servant. How came I by the favor of
this extraordinary visit?

SIR FRANCIS.

Ah, cousin!

MANLY.

Why that sorrowful face, man?   100

SIR FRANCIS.

I have no friend alive but you.

                    —123—

MANLY.

I am sorry for that—but what's the matter?

SIR FRANCIS.

I have played the fool by this journey, I see now; for my bitter wife—

MANLY.

What of her?   105

SIR FRANCIS.

Is playing the devil!

MANLY.

Why truly, that's a part that most of your fine ladies begin with, as soon as they get to London.

SIR FRANCIS.

If I am a living man, cousin, she has made away with above two hundred and fifty pound since yesterday 110 morning.

MANLY.

Hah, I see a good housewife will do a great deal of work in a little time.

SIR FRANCIS.

Work do they call it? Fine work indeed!

MANLY.

Well, but how do you mean, made away with it? What, 115 she has laid it out, maybe—but I suppose you have an account of it.

SIR FRANCIS.

Yes, yes, I have had the account, indeed; but I mun needs say, it's a verry sorry one.

MANLY.

Pray let's hear.   120

SIR FRANCIS.

Why, first, I let her have an hundred and fifty, to get things handsome about her, to let the world see that I was somebody. And I thought that sum was very genteel.

119. verry] *01–2*; very *03*.

---

119. *verry*] The spelling of 01–2 (see textual note) is possibly intended to suggest a dialect pronunciation.

MANLY.

Indeed I think so; and, in the country, might have
served her a twelvemonth.   125

SIR FRANCIS.

Why so it might—but here in this fine tawn, forsooth,
it could not get through four-and-twenty hours, for in
half that time it was all squandered away in baubles and
new-fashioned trumpery.

MANLY.

Oh, for ladies in London, Sir Francis, all this might be 130
necessary.

SIR FRANCIS.

Noa, theere's the plague on't! The devil o' one useful
thing do I see for it, but two pair of laced shoes,
and those stond me in three paund three shillings a
pair too.   135

MANLY.

Dear sir, this is nothing. Why we have City wives here
that, while their goodman is selling three pennyworth
of sugar, will give you twenty pound for a short apron.

SIR FRANCIS.

Mercy on us! What a mortal poor devil is a husband!

MANLY.

Well, but I hope you have nothing else to complain of? 140

SIR FRANCIS.

Ah, would I could say so too—but there's another hundred behind yet, that goes more to my heart than all
that went before it.

MANLY.

And how might that be disposed of?

SIR FRANCIS.

Troth, I am almost ashamed to tell you.   145

MANLY.

Out with it.

SIR FRANCIS.

Why, she has been at an assembly.

---

133. *laced shoes*] The most costly ladies' shoes were often decorated
with embroidery and gold thread.
137. *goodman*] husband.

MANLY.

> What, since I saw you? I thought you had all supped at
> home last night?

SIR FRANCIS.

> Why so we did, and all as merry as grigs. Ecod, my heart 150
> was so open that I tossed another hundred into her
> apron, to go out early this morning with. But the cloth
> was no sooner taken away than in comes my Lady
> Townly here (who between you and I—mum!—has had
> the devil to pay yonder) with another rantipole dame of 155
> quality, and out they must have her, they said, to intro-
> duce her at my Lady Noble's assembly, forsooth. A few
> words, you may be sure, made the bargain. So bawnce!
> and away they drive as if the devil had got into the
> coach box. So about four or five in the morning, home 160
> again comes madam, with her eyes a foot deep in her
> head, and my poor hundred pound left behind her at
> the hazard-table.

MANLY.

> All lost at dice!

SIR FRANCIS.

> Every shilling, among a parcel of pigtail puppies, and 165
> pale-faced women of quality.

MANLY.

> But pray, Sir Francis, how came you, after you found
> her so ill an housewife of one sum, so soon to trust
> her with another?

SIR FRANCIS.

> Why, truly, I mun say that was partly my own fault. 170
> For if I had not been a blab of my tongue, I believe
> that last hundred might have been saved.

MANLY.

> How so?

161. again] *01–2; om. 03.*

---

150. *as merry as grigs*] a proverbial phrase; a *grig* or *merry grig*
is an extravagantly lively, frolicsome person.
155. *rantipole*] wild, rakish.
157–158. *A few words . . . bargain*] a variant of the proverbial
phrase "Two words (to) make a bargain."
165. *pigtail puppies*] beaus wearing queue-wigs (see note to III.331).

SIR FRANCIS.

Why, like an owl (as I was), out of goodwill, forsooth,
partly to keep her in humor, I must needs tell her of 175
the thousand pound a year I had just got the promise
of. Ecod, she lays her claws upon it that moment—said it
was all owing to her advice, and truly she would have
her share on't.

MANLY.

What, before you had it yourself?   180

SIR FRANCIS.

Why aye, that's what I told her. "My dear," said I,
"mayhap I mayn't receive the first quarter on't this
half-year."

MANLY.

Sir Francis, I have heard you with a great deal of patience, and I really feel compassion for you.   185

SIR FRANCIS.

Truly, and well you may, cousin, for I don't see that my
wife's goodness is a bit the better for bringing to
London.

MANLY.

If you remember, I gave you a hint of it.

SIR FRANCIS.

Why aye, it's true you did so. But the devil himself 190
could not have believed she would have rid post to him.

MANLY.

Sir, if you stay but a fortnight in this town, you will
every day see hundreds as fast upon the gallop as she is.

SIR FRANCIS.

Ah, this London is a base place indeed. Waunds, if
things should happen to go wrong with me at West- 195
minster, at this rate, how the devil shall I keep out of
a jail?

MANLY.

Why truly, there seems to me but one way to avoid it.

SIR FRANCIS.

Ah, would you could tell me that, cousin.

194. a] *03; om. 01–2.*

MANLY.

The way lies plain before you, sir: the same road that 200
brought you hither will carry you safe home again.

SIR FRANCIS.

Od's flesh, cousin! What, and leave a thousand pound
a year behind me?

MANLY.

Pooh, pooh, leave anything behind you but your family,
and you are a saver by it.   205

SIR FRANCIS.

Aye, but consider, cousin, what a scurvy figure shall I
make in the country, if I come dawn withawt it.

MANLY.

You will make a much more lamentable figure in a jail
without it.

SIR FRANCIS.

Mayhap 'at yow have no great opinion of it then, 210
cousin?

MANLY.

Sir Francis, to do you the service of a real friend, I
must speak very plainly to you: you don't yet see half
the ruin that's before you.

SIR FRANCIS.

Good lack, how may yow mean, cousin?   215

MANLY.

In one word, your whole affairs stand thus: in a week,
you will lose your seat at Westminster; in a fortnight,
my lady will run you into a jail, by keeping the best
company; in four and twenty hours, your daughter will
run away with a sharper, because she has not been used 220
to better company, and your son will steal into marriage
with a cast mistress, because he has not been used to
any company at all.

SIR FRANCIS.

I' th' name o' goodness, why should you think all this?

MANLY.

Because I have proof of it. In short, I know so much of 225

---

222. *cast*] discarded.

their secrets that if all this is not prevented tonight,
it will be out of your power to do it tomorrow morning.

SIR FRANCIS.

Mercy upon us, you frighten me. Well sir, I will be
governed by yow. But what am I to do in this case?

MANLY.

I have not time here to give you proper instructions. But 230
about eight this evening I'll call at your lodgings, and
there you shall have full conviction how much I have
it at heart to serve you.

Enter a Servant.

SERVANT.

Sir, my lord desires to speak with you.

MANLY.

I'll wait upon him.   [*Exit* Servant.] 235

SIR FRANCIS.

Well then, I'll go straight home naw.

MANLY.

At eight depend upon me.

SIR FRANCIS.

Ah, dear cousin, I shall be bound to you as long as I
live. Mercy deliver us, what a terrible journey have I
made on't!   *Exeunt severally* 240

[V. ii]   *The scene opens to a dressing room.*
        Lady Townly, *as just up, walks to her toilet,*
                leaning on Mrs. Trusty.

MRS. TRUSTY.

Dear madam, what should make your ladyship so out
of order?

LADY TOWNLY.

How is it possible to be well, where one is killed for
want of sleep?

MRS. TRUSTY.

Dear me, it was so long before you rung, madam, I   5
was in hopes your ladyship had been finely composed.

[V.ii]
  0.2. *toilet*] dressing table.

LADY TOWNLY.

Composed! Why, I have lain in an inn here; this house
is worse than an inn with ten stagecoaches. What
between my lord's impertinent people of business in
a morning, and the intolerable thick shoes of footmen   10
at noon, one has not a wink all night.

MRS. TRUSTY.

Indeed, madam, it's a great pity my lord can't be persuaded into the hours of people of quality. Though I
must say that, madam, your ladyship is certainly the
best matrimonial menager in town.   15

LADY TOWNLY.

Oh, you are quite mistaken, Trusty, I menage very ill;
for notwithstanding all the power I have, by never being
overfond of my lord, yet I want money infinitely oftener
than he is willing to give it me.

MRS. TRUSTY.

Ah, if his lordship could but be brought to play him-   20
self, madam, then he might feel what it is to want
money.

LADY TOWNLY.

Oh, don't talk of it! Do you know that I am undone,
Trusty?

MRS. TRUSTY.

Mercy forbid, madam!   25

LADY TOWNLY.

Broke, ruined, plundered! Stripped, even to a confisca-
tion of my last guinea.

MRS. TRUSTY.

You don't tell me so, madam!

LADY TOWNLY.

And where to raise ten pound in the world—what is to
be done, Trusty?   30

8. is] *03*; in *01–2*.   15. menager] *01–2*; manager *03*.
                                 16. menage] *01–2*; manage *03*.

---

15. *menager*] one who runs the household (*ménage*) and gets her
own way. Cibber was fond of spelling manager with an "e" (see
Apology, passim), but since 01–2 elsewhere have *management* (I.410–
411) and *managed* (III.257), it seems likely that Mrs. Trusty's *menager*
and Lady Townly's *menage* (l.16) are modish Gallicisms.

MRS. TRUSTY.

Truly, I wish I were wise enough to tell you, madam.
But maybe your ladyship may have a run of better fortune upon some of the good company that comes here
tonight.

LADY TOWNLY.

But I have not a single guinea, to try my fortune.   35

MRS. TRUSTY.

Ha, that's a bad business indeed, madam. —Adad, I have
a thought in my head, madam, if it is not too late—

LADY TOWNLY.

Out with it quickly then, I beseech thee.

MRS. TRUSTY.

Has not the steward something of fifty pound, madam,
that you left in his hands to pay somebody about this   40
time?

LADY TOWNLY.

Oh, aye, I had forgot. 'Twas to—a—what's his filthy
name?

MRS. TRUSTY.

Now I remember, madam, 'twas to Mr. Lutestring your
old mercer, that your ladyship turned off about a year   45
ago because he would trust you no longer.

LADY TOWNLY.

The very wretch! If he has not paid it, run quickly,
dear Trusty, and bid him bring it hither immediately.

Exit Mrs. Trusty.

Well, sure mortal woman never had such fortune! Five,

---

36. *Adad*] probably a variant of "egad."
44. *Lutestring*] fine corded silk.
45. *mercer*] supplier of textiles, especially silks.
49–50. *Five . . . forever*] In hazard the "caster" calls a number
between five and nine, which then becomes the "main"; he tries to
throw this main with the two dice and so win the stakes. Against a
main of seven (the one most usually called, since the odds favor its
being thrown) he may for example throw an eight. This constitutes
a *chance*; he can win by throwing his *chance* again, but if he now
throws the main he loses and must pay out whatever has been staked
against him. Lady Townly has only succeeded in throwing chances of
five and nine against the main of seven, and has repeatedly failed
to clinch her game.

five, and nine, against poor seven forever! No, after 50
that horrid bar of my chance, that Lady Wronghead's
fatal red fist upon the table, I saw it was impossible ever
to win another stake. Sit up all night; lose all one's
money; dream of winning thousands; wake without a
shilling, and *then*—how like a hag I look! In short, the 55
pleasures of life are not worth this disorder. If it were
not for shame now, I could almost think my Lady
Grace's sober scheme not quite so ridiculous. If my wise
lord could but hold his tongue for a week, 'tis odds
but I should hate the town in a fortnight. But I will not 60
be driven out of it, that's positive!

Mrs. Trusty returns.

MRS. TRUSTY.

Oh madam, there is no bearing it! Mr. Lutestring was
just let in at the door as I came to the stair-foot, and
the steward is now actually paying him the money in
the hall.   65

LADY TOWNLY.

Run to the staircase head again, and scream to him that
I must speak with him this instant.

Mrs. Trusty runs out, and speaks.

MRS. TRUSTY.

Mr. Poundage, ahem! Mr. Poundage, a word with you
quickly.

POUNDAGE (*within*).

I'll come to you presently.   70

MRS. TRUSTY.

Presently won't do, man, you must come this minute.

POUNDAGE.

I am but just paying a little money here.

MRS. TRUSTY.

Cod's my life! Paying money? Is the man distracted?
Come here I tell you, to my lady, this moment, quick!

50–52. *after that . . . table*] Perhaps it was thought to bring the
caster bad luck if another player touched the table while play was
in progress. Lady Wronghead does not know the etiquette of hazard
and blights Lady Townly's game.
64. *actually*] at this very moment.

Mrs. Trusty *returns.*

LADY TOWNLY.

Will the monster come, or no?   75

MRS. TRUSTY.

Yes, I hear him now, madam; he is hobbling up as fast
as he can.

LADY TOWNLY.

Don't let him come in, for he will keep such a babbling
about his accounts—my brain is not able to bear him.

> Poundage *comes to the door with*
> *a moneybag in his hand.*

MRS. TRUSTY.

Oh, it's well you are come, sir. Where's the fifty pound? 80

POUNDAGE.

Why here it is. If you had not been in such haste I
should have paid it by this time; the man's now writing
a receipt, below, for it.

MRS. TRUSTY.

No matter. My lady says you must not pay him with
that money, there is not enough, it seems; there's a   85
pistole, and a guinea that is not good in it. Besides
there is a mistake in the account too. (*Twitching the
bag from him.*) But she is not at leisure to examine it
now, so you must bid Mr. What-d'ye-call-um call another
time.   90

LADY TOWNLY.

What is all that noise there?

POUNDAGE.

Why and it please your ladyship—

LADY TOWNLY.

Prithee, don't plague me now, but do as you were
ordered.

POUNDAGE.

Nay, what your ladyship pleases, madam—   95

> *Exit* Poundage.

---

86. *pistole*] a Spanish gold coin, though the name was also given
to the French *louis d'or*. Both coins were worth rather less than a
guinea.

MRS. TRUSTY.

There they are, madam. (*Pours the money out of the bag.*) The pretty things—were so near falling into a nasty tradesman's hands, I protest it made me tremble for them. I fancy your ladyship had as good give me that bad guinea, for luck's sake—thank you madam.   100
Takes a guinea.

LADY TOWNLY.

Why, I did not bid you take it.

MRS. TRUSTY.

No, but your ladyship looked as if you were just going to bid me, and so I was willing to save you the trouble of speaking, madam.

LADY TOWNLY.

Well, thou hast deserved it, and so for once—but hark! 105 don't I hear the man making a noise yonder? Though I think now we may compound for a little of his ill humor—

MRS. TRUSTY.

I'll listen.

LADY TOWNLY.

Prithee do.   Mrs. Trusty *goes to the door.* 110

MRS. TRUSTY.

Aye, they are at it, madam. He is in a bitter passion with poor Poundage. Bless me, I believe he'll beat him. Mercy on us, how the wretch swears!

LADY TOWNLY.

And a sober citizen too; that's a shame!

MRS. TRUSTY.

Hah, I think all's silent of a sudden. Maybe the porter 115 has knocked him down. I'll step and see.   *Exit Mrs. Trusty.*

LADY TOWNLY.

Those tradespeople are the troublesomest creatures; no words will satisfy them.

Mrs. Trusty *returns.*

---

107. *compound for*] settle for, accept in return for our treatment of him.
115. *porter*] the doorkeeper employed by wealthy families.

MRS. TRUSTY.

Oh madam, undone, undone! My lord has just bolted
out upon the man, and is hearing all his pitiful story 120
over. If your ladyship pleases to come hither you may
hear him yourself.

LADY TOWNLY.

No matter, it will come round presently. I shall have it
all from my lord, without losing a word by the way, I'll
warrant you.   125

MRS. TRUSTY.

Oh lud, madam, here's my lord just coming in.

LADY TOWNLY.

Do you get out of the way then.   *Exit* Mrs. Trusty.
I am afraid I want spirits; but he will soon give 'em me.

Enter Lord Townly.

LORD TOWNLY.

How comes it, madam, that a tradesman dares be clam-
orous, in my house, for money due to him from you?   130

LADY TOWNLY.

You don't expect, my lord, that I should answer for
other people's impertinence?

LORD TOWNLY.

I expect, madam, you should answer for your own ex-
travagances, that are the occasion of it. I thought I had
given you money three months ago to satisfy all these 135
sort of people.

LADY TOWNLY.

Yes, but you see they never *are* to be satisfied.

LORD TOWNLY.

Nor am I, madam, longer to be abused thus. What's
become of the last five hundred I gave you?

LADY TOWNLY.

Gone.   140

LORD TOWNLY.

Gone! What way, madam?

LADY TOWNLY.

Half the town over, I believe, by this time.

LORD TOWNLY.

'Tis well! I see ruin will make no impression till it falls upon *you*.

LADY TOWNLY.

In short, my lord, if money is always the subject of our 145 conversation, I shall make you no answer.

LORD TOWNLY.

Madam, madam, I will be heard, and *make* you answer.

LADY TOWNLY.

Make me? Then I must tell you, my lord, this is a language I have not been used to, and I won't bear it.

LORD TOWNLY.

Come, come, madam, you shall bear a great deal more, 150 before I part with you.

LADY TOWNLY.

My lord, if you insult me, you will have as much to bear on your side, I can assure you.

LORD TOWNLY.

Pooh, your spirit grows ridiculous; you have neither honor, worth, or innocence to support it.   155

LADY TOWNLY.

You'll find, at least, I have resentment; and do you look well to the provocation!

LORD TOWNLY.

After those you have given me, madam, 'tis almost infamous to talk with you.

LADY TOWNLY.

I scorn your imputation, and your menaces. The nar- 160 rowness of your heart's your monitor. 'Tis there, there, my lord, you are wounded; you have less to complain of than many husbands of an equal rank to you.

LORD TOWNLY.

Death, madam, do you presume upon your corporal merit? That your person's less tainted than your mind? 165 Is it there, there alone an honest husband can be

---

156–157. *look well to*] beware of giving.

160–161. *The narrowness . . . monitor*] Your ungenerous, parsimonious nature regulates all your conduct, and makes you suspicious of others.

injured? Have you not every other vice that can debase
your birth, or stain the heart of woman? Is not your
health, your beauty, husband, fortune, family disclaimed,
for nights consumed in riot and extravagance? The 170
wanton does no more; if she conceals her shame, does
less. And sure the dissolute avowed, as sorely wrongs my
honor and my quiet.

LADY TOWNLY.

I see, my lord, what sort of wife might please you.

LORD TOWNLY.

Ungrateful woman! Could you have seen yourself, you 175
in yourself had seen her. I am amazed our legislature
has left no precedent of a divorce for this more visible
injury, this adultery of the mind, as well as that of the
person. When a woman's whole heart is alienated to
pleasures I have no share in, what is't to me whether a 180
black ace, or a powdered coxcomb, has possession of it?

LADY TOWNLY.

If you have not found it yet, my lord, this is not the
way to get possession of mine, depend upon it.

LORD TOWNLY.

That, madam, I have long despaired of; and since our
happiness cannot be mutual, 'tis fit that with our hearts, 185
our persons too should separate. This house you sleep no
more in! Though your content might grossly feed upon
the dishonor of a husband, yet my desires would starve
upon the features of a wife.

LADY TOWNLY.

Your style, my lord, is much of the same delicacy with 190
your sentiments of honor.

LORD TOWNLY.

Madam, madam, this is no time for compliments. I have
done with you.

LADY TOWNLY.

If we had never met, my lord, I had not broke my heart

---

181. *black ace*] In ombre and quadrille the ace of spades, being the
highest trump, is the most powerful card.
181. *powdered*] Fops perfumed both their wigs and their coats,
especially about the shoulders, with sweet-scented powder.

for it. But have a care! I may not, perhaps, be so easily 195
recalled as you imagine.

LORD TOWNLY.

Recalled! —Who's there?

Enter a Servant.

Desire my sister and Mr. Manly to walk up.   [*Exit* Servant.]

LADY TOWNLY.

My lord, you may proceed as you please, but pray what
indiscretions have I committed that are not daily prac- 200
ticed by a hundred other women of quality?

LORD TOWNLY.

'Tis not the number of ill wives, madam, that makes the
patience of a husband less contemptible; and though a
bad one may be the best man's lot, yet he'll make a
better figure in the world that keeps his misfortune out 205
of doors, than he that tamely keeps her within.

LADY TOWNLY.

I don't know what figure you may make, my lord, but I
shall have no reason to be ashamed of mine, in whatever
company I may meet you.

LORD TOWNLY.

Be sparing of your spirit, madam, you'll need it to sup- 210
port you.

Enter Lady Grace *and* Manly.

Mr. Manly, I have an act of friendship to beg of you
which wants more apologies than words can make for it.

MANLY.

Then pray make none, my lord, that I may have the
greater merit in obliging you.   215

LORD TOWNLY.

Sister, I have the same excuse to entreat of you too.

LADY GRACE.

To your request, I beg, my lord.

LORD TOWNLY.

Thus then: as you both were present at my ill-considered
marriage, I now desire you each will be a witness of my

205. misfortune] *01–2;* misfortunes
03.

determined separation. I know, sir, your good nature, 220
and my sister's, must be shocked at the office I impose
on you. But, as I don't ask your justification of my cause,
so I hope you are conscious that an ill woman can't
reproach you, if you are silent upon her side.

MANLY.

My lord, I never thought, till now. it could be difficult 225
to oblige you.

LADY GRACE (*aside*).

Heavens, how I tremble!

LORD TOWNLY.

For you, my Lady Townly, I need not here repeat the
provocations of my parting with you; the world, I fear,
is too well informed of them. For the good lord, your 230
dead father's sake, I will still support you, as his daughter. As the Lord Townly's wife, you have had everything
a fond husband could bestow, and (to our mutual shame
I speak it) more than happy wives desire. But those
indulgencies must end. State, equipage, and splendor 235
but ill become the vices that misuse 'em. The decent
necessaries of life shall be supplied—but not one article
to luxury! Not even the coach, that waits to carry you
from hence, shall you ever use again. Your tender aunt,
my Lady Lovemore, with tears this morning has con- 240
sented to receive you; where if time and your condition
brings you to a due reflection, your allowance shall be
increased. But if you still are lavish of your little, or
pine for past licentious pleasures, that little shall be less!
Nor will I call that soul my friend, that names you in my 245
hearing!

LADY GRACE (*aside*).

My heart bleeds for her!

LORD TOWNLY.

Oh Manly, look there! Turn back thy thoughts with me,
and witness to my growing love. There was a time when
I believed that form incapable of vice, or of decay. There 250
I proposed the partner of an easy home. There I, for-

223. an] *03*; *om. 01–2.*

---

235. *equipage*] all the trappings of high life.

ever, hoped to find a cheerful companion, an agreeable
intimate, a faithful friend, a useful helpmate, and a
tender mother. But oh, how bitter now the disappointment.   255

MANLY.

The world is different in its sense of happiness. Offended
as you are, I know you will still be just.

LORD TOWNLY.

Fear me not.

MANLY *(aside)*.

This last reproach, I see, has struck her.

LORD TOWNLY.

No, let me not (though I this moment cast her from my   260
heart forever), let me not urge her punishment beyond
her crimes. I know the world is fond of any tale that
feeds its appetite of scandal; and as I am conscious
severities of this kind seldom fail of imputations too
gross to mention, I here, before you both, acquit her   265
of the least suspicion raised against the honor of my bed.
Therefore, when abroad her conduct may be questioned,
do her fame that justice.

LADY TOWNLY.

Oh sister!   *Turns to* Lady Grace *weeping.*

LORD TOWNLY.

When I am spoken of, where without favor this action   270
may be canvassed, relate but half my provocations, and
give me up to censure.   *Going.*

LADY TOWNLY.

Support me, save me, hide me from the world!
                              Falls on Lady Grace's *neck.*

LORD TOWNLY *(returning)*.

I had forgot me. You have no share in my resentment;
therefore, as you have lived in friendship with her,   275
your parting may admit of gentler terms than suit the
honor of an injured husband.   *Offers to go out.*

MANLY *(interposing)*.

My lord, you must not, shall not leave her thus! One

---

272. *give . . . censure*] let people form their own judgments about
my conduct.

moment's stay can do your cause no wrong. If looks can
speak the anguish of the heart, I'll answer with my life 280
there's something laboring in her mind that, would you
bear the hearing, might deserve it.

LORD TOWNLY.

Consider! Since we no more can meet, press not my
staying, to insult her.

LADY TOWNLY.

Yet stay, my lord. The little I would say will not deserve 285
an insult; and undeserved, I know your nature gives it
not. But as you've called in friends to witness your
resentment, let them be equal hearers of my last reply.

LORD TOWNLY.

I shan't refuse you that, madam. Be it so.

LADY TOWNLY.

My lord, you ever have complained I wanted love; but 290
as you kindly have allowed I never gave it to another,
so when you hear the story of my heart, though you
may still complain, you will not wonder at my coldness.

LADY GRACE (apart).

This promises a reverse of temper.

MANLY.

This, my lord, you are concerned to hear! 295

LORD TOWNLY.

Proceed, I am attentive.

LADY TOWNLY.

Before I was your bride, my lord, the flattering world
had talked me into beauty—which, at my glass, my youthful vanity confirmed. Wild with that fame, I thought
mankind my slaves. I triumphed over hearts, while all 300
my pleasure was their pain. Yet was my own so equally
insensible to all, that when a father's firm commands
enjoined me to make choice of one, I even there declined
the liberty he gave, and to his own election yielded up
my youth. His tender care, my lord, directed him to you. 305
Our hands were joined, but still my heart was wedded
to its folly. My only joy was power, command, society,
profuseness, and to lead in pleasures. The husband's
right to rule I thought a vulgar law, which only the de-
formed or meanly-spirited obeyed. I knew no directors 310

but my passions, no master but my will. Even you, my
lord, sometime o'ercome by love, were pleased with my
delights, nor then foresaw this mad misuse of your indulgence. And, though I call myself ungrateful while I
own it, yet as a truth it cannot be denied—that kind 315
indulgence has undone me! It added strength to my
habitual failings, and in a heart thus warm in wild
unthinking life, no wonder if the gentler sense of love
was lost.

LORD TOWNLY (apart).
   Oh Manly, where has this creature's heart been buried? 320

MANLY.
   If yet recoverable—how vast a treasure!

LADY TOWNLY.
   What I have said, my lord, is not my excuse, but my
confession. My errors (give 'em, if you please, a harder
name) cannot be defended. No! What's in its nature
wrong, no words can palliate, no plea can alter. What 325
then remains, in my condition, but resignation to your
pleasure? Time only can convince you of my future conduct. Therefore, till I have lived an object of forgive-
ness, I dare not hope for pardon. The penance of a
lonely contrite life were little to the innocent; but to 330
have deserved this separation will strow perpetual thorns
upon my pillow.

LADY GRACE.
   Oh happy, heavenly hearing!

LADY TOWNLY.
   Sister, farewell. (Kissing her.) Your virtue needs no
warning from the shame that falls on me. But when you 335
think I have atoned my follies past—persuade your
injured brother to forgive them.

LORD TOWNLY.
   No, madam! Your errors thus renounced, this instant are
forgotten. So deep, so due a sense of them has made
you—what my utmost wishes formed, and all my heart 340
has sighed for.

LADY TOWNLY (turning to Lady Grace).
   How odious does this goodness make me!

LADY GRACE.

How amiable your thinking so!

LORD TOWNLY.

Long-parted friends, that pass through easy voyages of
life, receive but common gladness in their meeting; but 345
from a shipwreck saved, we mingle tears with our em-
braces.   *Embracing* Lady Townly.

LADY TOWNLY.

What words, what love, what duty can repay such
obligations?

LORD TOWNLY.

Preserve but this desire to please, your power is endless. 350

LADY TOWNLY.

Oh, till this moment never did I know, my lord, I had
a heart to give you.

LORD TOWNLY.

By heaven, this yielding hand, when first it gave you
to my wishes, presented not a treasure more desirable!
Oh Manly, sister, as you have often shared in my dis- 355
quiet, partake of my felicity, my new-born joy. See here
the bride of my desires. This may be called my wedding
day!

LADY GRACE.

Sister (for now methinks that name is dearer to my heart
than ever), let me congratulate the happiness that opens 360
to you.

MANLY.

Long, long, and mutual may it flow—

LORD TOWNLY.

To make our happiness complete, my dear, join here
with me to give a hand that amply will repay the
obligation.   365

LADY TOWNLY.

Sister, a day like this—

LADY GRACE.

Admits of no excuse against the general joy.
                                    Gives her hand to Manly.

MANLY.

A joy like mine—despairs of words to speak it.

LORD TOWNLY (*embracing him*).

Oh Manly, how the name of friend endears the brother!

MANLY.

Your words, my lord, will warm me to deserve them.   370

Enter a Servant.

SERVANT.

My lord, the apartments are full of masqueraders, and
some people of quality there desire to see your lordship,
and my lady.

LADY TOWNLY.

I thought, my lord, your orders had forbid this revelling?

LORD TOWNLY.

No, my dear, Manly has desired their admittance tonight,   375
it seems upon a particular occasion. —Say we will wait
upon them instantly.   *Exit* Servant.

LADY TOWNLY.

I shall be but ill company to them.

LORD TOWNLY.

No matter. Not to see them would, on a sudden, be too
particular. Lady Grace will assist you to entertain them.   380

LADY TOWNLY.

With her, my lord, I shall be always easy. —Sister, to
your unerring virtue I now commit the guidance of my
future days.

> Never the paths of pleasure more to tread,
> But where your guarded innocence shall lead.   385
> For in the married state, the world must own,
> Divided happiness was never known.
> To make it mutual, Nature points the way:
> Let husbands govern, gentle wives obey.   *Exeunt.*

[V.iii]

*The scene, opening to another apartment, discovers
a great number of people in masquerade, talking all
together, and playing upon one another:* Lady Wrong-

---

376. *particular*] It would look odd and excite comment.
[V.iii]
0.3. *playing upon*] making fun of, mocking.

head *as a shepherdess,* Jenny *as a nun, the* Squire *as a running footman, and the* Count *in a domino. After some time,* Lord *and* Lady Townly, *with* Lady Grace, *enter to them unmasked.*

LORD TOWNLY.

So, here's a great deal of company.

LADY GRACE.

A great many people, my lord, but no company—as you'll find, for here's one now that seems to have a mind to entertain us.

A Mask, *after some affected gesture,*
makes up to Lady Townly.

MASK.

Well, my dear Lady Townly, shan't we see you by and   5
by?

LADY TOWNLY.

I don't know you, madam.

MASK *(in a squeaking tone).*

Don't you, seriously?

LADY TOWNLY.

Not I, indeed.

MASK.

Well, that's charming! But can't you guess?   10

LADY TOWNLY.

Yes, I could guess wrong, I believe.

MASK.

That's what I'd have you do.

LADY TOWNLY.

But madam, if I don't know you at all, is not that as well?

0.5. *running footman*] a servant employed to carry messages, and run before his master's carriage to give notice of his arrival. "They wear fine Holland drawers and waistcoats, thread stockings, a blue silk sash fringed with silver, a velvet cap with a great tassel; and carry a Porter's staff with a large silver handle" (James P. Malcolm, *Anecdotes of the Manners and Customs of London during the Eighteenth Century* [London, 1808], p. 432, quoting a description of 1730).

0.5. *domino*] a kind of loose cloak, its design based on the dress of Venetian noblemen. It was usually worn by those who did not wish to take an active part in the mask.

MASK.

    Aye, but you do know me.   15

LADY TOWNLY (*apart*).

    Dear sister, take her off o' my hands; there's no bearing this.

LADY GRACE.

    I fancy I know you, madam.

MASK.

    I fancy you don't. What makes you think you do?

LADY GRACE.

    Because I have heard you talk.   20

MASK.

    Aye, but you don't know my voice, I'm sure.

LADY GRACE.

    There is something in your wit and humor, madam, so very much your own, it is impossible you can be anybody but my Lady Trifle.

MASK (*unmasking*).

    Dear Lady Grace, thou art a charming creature.   25

LADY GRACE.

    Is there nobody else we know here?

MASK.

    Oh dear, yes! I have found out fifty already.

LADY GRACE.

    Pray, who are they?

MASK.

    Oh, charming company! There's Lady Ramble—Lady Riot—Lady Kill-care—Lady Squander—Lady Strip—Lady 30 Pawn—and the Duchess of Single-guinea.

LORD TOWNLY (*apart*).

    Is not it hard, my dear, that people of sense and probity are sometimes forced to seem fond of such company?

LADY TOWNLY.

    My lord, it will always give me pain to remember their acquaintance, but none to drop it immediately.   35

LADY GRACE [*to the* Mask].

    But you have given us no account of the men, madam. Are they good for anything?

27. found out] *01–2*; out found out *03*.

MASK.

Oh yes. You must know, I always find out them by their
endeavors to find out me.

LADY GRACE.

Pray, who are they?   40

MASK.

Why, for your men of tip-top wit and pleasure, about
town, there's my Lord Bite—Lord Arch-wag—young
Brazen-Wit—Lord Timberdown—Lord Joint-life—and—
Lord Mortgage. Then, for your pretty fellows only,
there's Sir Powder Peacock—Lord Lapwing—Billy Mag-   45
pie—Beau Frightful—Sir Paul Plaster-crown, and the
Marquess of Monkey-man.

LADY GRACE.

Right! And these are the fine gentlemen that never
want elbow-room at an assembly.

MASK.

The rest, I suppose, by their tawdry, hired habits, are   50
tradesmen's wives, Inns-of-Court beaus, Jews, and kept
mistresses.

LORD TOWNLY.

An admirable collection!

LADY GRACE.

Well, of all our public diversions, I am amazed how
this that is so very expensive, and has so little to show   55
for it, can draw so much company together.

LORD TOWNLY.

Oh, if it were not expensive the better sort would not
come into it; and because money can purchase a ticket,
the common people scorn to be kept out of it.

---

42. *Bite*] cheat, sharper.

43. *Timberdown*] His name makes the stock joke against irresponsible landowners who sold valuable timber in order to buy finery.

43. *Joint-life*] deriving his income from an annuity taken on two
or more joint lives. Such an annuity is necessarily less valuable than
one on a single life.

45. *Lapwing*] a bird which carries a conspicuous crest on its head.
In his *Apology* Cibber speaks of beaus who emulate "the pert Air of
a Lapwing" (p. 202).

46. *Plaster-crown*] Pomade, or scented ointment, was used to dress
elaborately curled wigs.

MASK.

> Right, my lord. Poor Lady Grace! I suppose you are   60
> under the same astonishment that an opera should draw
> so much good company.

LADY GRACE.

> Not at all, madam; it's an easier matter sure to gratify
> the ear than the understanding. But have you no notion,
> madam, of receiving pleasure and profit at the same   65
> time?

MASK.

> Oh, quite none—unless it be sometimes winning a great
> stake. Laying down, a *vole sans prendre* may come up,
> to the profitable pleasure you were speaking of.

LORD TOWNLY *(apart)*.

> You seem attentive, my dear.   70

LADY TOWNLY.

> I am, my lord, and amazed at my own follies, so strongly
> painted in another woman.

LADY GRACE.

> But see, my lord, we had best adjourn our debate, I
> believe, for here are some masks that seem to have a
> mind to divert other people as well as themselves.   75

LORD TOWNLY.

> The least we can do is to give them a clear stage then.

A dance of Masks here, in various characters.

This was a favor extraordinary.

Enter Manly.

Oh Manly, I thought we had lost you.

68. Laying down, a *vole*] *this edn.*; laying down a *vole, O1–3.*

---

68. *Laying down . . . come up*] i.e., "having made your wager (laid down your stake), you may find yourself holding cards that will sweep the board." At quadrille, to win the *vole* is to take all ten tricks; to play *sans prendre* is to play solo, and therefore to win all the stakes. (The original punctuation, recorded in the textual note, does not yield any very satisfactory sense.)

MANLY.

    I ask pardon, my lord, but I have been obliged to look a
little after my country family.   80

LORD TOWNLY.

    Well, pray, what have you done with them?

MANLY.

    They are all in the house here, among the masks, my
lord. If your lordship has curiosity enough to step into
a lower apartment, in three minutes I'll give you an
ample account of them.   85

LORD TOWNLY.

    Oh, by all means. We will wait upon you.

       [*Exeunt* Lord *and* Lady Townly, Lady Grace, Manly.]

[V. iv]   *The scene shuts upon the Masks, to a*
               smaller apartment.
    Manly *re-enters, with* Sir Francis Wronghead.

SIR FRANCIS.

    Well, cousin, you have made my very hair stand
an-end! Waunds, if what you tell me be true, I'll stuff
my whole family into a stagecoach, and trundle them
into the country again on Monday morning.

MANLY.

    Stick to that, sir, and we may yet find a way to redeem   5
all. In the meantime place yourself behind this screen,
and for the truth of what I have told you, take the evidence of your own senses. But be sure you keep close
till I give you the signal.

SIR FRANCIS.

    Sir, I'll warrant you. Ah, my lady, my Lady Wronghead!   10
What a bitter business have you drawn me into!

MANLY.

    Hush, to your post. Here comes one couple already.

       Sir Francis *retires behind the screen. Exit* Manly.

     Enter Myrtilla, *with* Squire Richard.

[V.iv]
   2. *an-end*] upright (not a low or dialect word, but an acceptable
alternative to "on end").

SQUIRE RICHARD.

What, is this the doctor's chamber?

MYRTILLA.

Yes, yes; speak softly.

SQUIRE RICHARD.

Well, but where is he? 15

MYRTILLA.

He'll be ready for us presently, but he says he can't do
us the good turn without witnesses. So when the count
and your sister come, you know, he and you may be
fathers for one another.

SQUIRE RICHARD.

Well, well, tit for tat. Aye, aye, that will be friendly. 20

MYRTILLA.

And see, here they come.

Enter Count Basset *and* Miss Jenny.

COUNT BASSET.

So, so, here's your brother and his bride before us, my
dear.

JENNY.

Well, I vow my heart's at my mouth still. I thought I
should never have got rid of mamma; but while she 25
stood gaping upon the dance I gave her the slip. Lawd!
do but feel how it beats here.

COUNT BASSET.

Oh, the pretty flutterer! I protest, my dear, you have
put mine into the same palpitation.

JENNY.

Ah, you say so, but let's see now—oh lud, I vow it thumps 30
purely. Well, well, I see it will do, and so where's the
parson?

COUNT BASSET.

Mrs. Myrtilla, will you be so good as to see if the doctor's
ready for us?

MYRTILLA.

He only stayed for you, sir. I'll fetch him immediately. 35

Exit Myrtilla.

JENNY.

Pray sir, am not I to take place of mamma when I'm a
countess?

COUNT BASSET.

No doubt on't, my dear.

JENNY.

Oh lud, how her back will be up then, when she meets
me at an assembly, or you and I in our coach-and-six   40
at Hyde Park together!

COUNT BASSET.

Aye, or when she hears the box-keepers, at an opera, call
out: "The Countess of Basset's servants!"

JENNY.

Well, I say it, that will be delicious. And then, mayhap,
to have a fine gentleman with a star and a what-d'ye-   45
call-um ribbon lead me to my chair, with his hat under
his arm all the way. "Hold up," says the chair-man. "And
so," says I, "my lord, your humble servant." "I suppose,
madam," says he, "we shall see you at my Lady Quadrille's." "Aye, aye, to be sure, my lord," says I. So in   50
swops me, with my hoop stuffed up to my forehead, and
away they trot, swing! swang! with my tassels dangling,
and my flambeaux blazing, and—oh, it's a charming
thing to be a woman of quality!

COUNT BASSET.

Well, I see that plainly, my dear, there's ne'er a duchess   55
of 'em all will become an equipage like you.

JENNY.

Well, well, do you find equipage, and I'll find airs, I
warrant you.

51. swops me] *03*; troops I *01-2*.

---

36. *place*] social precedence.
41. *Hyde Park*] popular with the nobility and gentry as a place
for evening drives.
42. *box-keepers*] attendants at theater boxes.
51. *swops me*] "I plump myself down." The discarded reading of
01-2 (*troop* = walk, pass) is not so comically forceful.
51. *hoop . . . forehead*] The hooped skirt, with its whalebone frame-
work, was an encumbrance when traveling.
52. *tassels*] decorating the outer corners of the sedan-chair roof.

Sings.

What though they call me country lass,
I read it plainly in my glass   60
That for a duchess I might pass—
    Oh, could I see the day!
Would Fortune but attend my call,
At park, at play, at Ring, and ball,
I'd brave the proudest of them all,   65
    With a "Stand by—clear the way."

Surrounded by a crowd of beaus,
With smart toupees and powdered clothes,
At rivals I'll turn up my nose—
    Oh, could I see the day!   70
I'll dart such glances from these eyes,
Shall make some lord, or duke, my prize;
And then, oh, how I'll tyrannize,
    With a "Stand by—clear the way."

Oh, then for every new delight,   75
For equipage and diamonds bright,
Quadrille, and plays, and balls, all night—
    Oh, could I see the day!
Of love and joy I'd take my fill,
The tedious hours of life to kill,   80
In everything I'd have my will,
    With a "Stand by—clear the way."

58.1. *Sings*] *03 (which prints the
text of the song after the Epilogue); om. 01-2.*

---

64. *Ring*] a fenced circular drive in the highest part of Hyde Park.
"Here, in a fair Summer Day, towards the Evening, 'tis common to
see 2 or 300 Coaches . . . going gently about a Ring, for Gentlemen
and Ladies to have a View of each other, and at the same time breathe
the Air" (Guy Miège, *The Present State of Great Britain and Ireland*,
4th edn. [London, 1718], part I, p. 106).
66. *Stand by*] stand aside—the usual cry of servants when clearing
a path for their masters.
68. *toupees*] wigs with the front hair combed up into a curl or
topknot.

SQUIRE RICHARD.

Troth, I think this masquerading's the merriest game
that ever I saw in my life. Thof, in my mind, and there
were but a little wrestling, or cudgel-playing naw, it   85
would help it hugely. But what a rope makes the parson
stay so?

COUNT BASSET.

Oh here he comes, I believe.

Enter Myrtilla, *with a* Constable.

CONSTABLE.

Well madam, pray which is the party that wants a
spice of my office here?   90

MYRTILLA *(pointing to the* Count*)*.

That's the gentleman.

COUNT BASSET.

Hey-day! What, in masquerade, doctor?

CONSTABLE.

Doctor? Sir, I believe you have mistaken your man. But
if you are called Count Basset, I have a billet-doux in my
hand for you that will set you right presently.   95

COUNT BASSET.

What the devil's the meaning of all this?

CONSTABLE.

Only my Lord Chief Justice's warrant against you for
forgery, sir.

COUNT BASSET.

Blood and thunder!

CONSTABLE.

And so, sir, if you please to pull off your fool's frock 100
there, I'll wait upon you to the next Justice of Peace
immediately.

JENNY *(trembling)*.

Oh dear me, what's the matter?

---

85. *cudgel-playing*] a boisterous sport considered proper only for
country people and apprentices.
86. *what a rope*] a "low," rustic exclamation of anger and irritation.
The *rope* in question is the hangman's.
95. *presently*] here used in the already old-fashioned sense of "at
once."

COUNT BASSET.

Oh nothing, only a masquerading frolic, my dear.

SQUIRE RICHARD.

Oh ho, is that all?   105

SIR FRANCIS.

No sirrah, that is not all.

Sir Francis, coming softly behind the Squire, *knocks him down with his cane. Enter* Manly.

SQUIRE RICHARD.

Oh lawd, oh lawd! he has beaten my brains out.

MANLY.

Hold, hold, Sir Francis, have a little mercy upon my poor godson, pray sir.

SIR FRANCIS.

Waunds, cozen, I han't patience.   110

COUNT BASSET (*aside*).

Manly! Nay, then I am blown to the devil.

SQUIRE RICHARD.

Oh my head, my head!

Enter Lady Wronghead.

LADY WRONGHEAD.

What's the matter here, gentlemen? For heaven's sake! What, are you murdering my children?

CONSTABLE.

No, no, madam, no murther—only a little suspicion of 115
felony, that's all.

SIR FRANCIS (*to* Jenny).

And for you, Mrs. Hot-upon't, I could find in my heart to make you wear that habit as long as you live, you jade you. Do you know, hussy, that you were within two minutes of marrying a pickpocket?   120

COUNT BASSET (*aside*).

So, so, all's out, I find.

JENNY.

Oh the mercy! Why pray, papa, is not the count a man of quality then?

---

115. *murther*] another archaism.
118. *that habit*] i.e., her nun's costume.

SIR FRANCIS.

Oh yes, one of the unhanged ones, it seems.

LADY WRONGHEAD (*aside*).

Married! Oh, the confident thing! There was his urgent 125
business then—slighted for her! I han't patience! And
for aught I know, I have been all this while making a
friendship with a highwayman!

MANLY.

Mr. Constable, secure that door there.

SIR FRANCIS.

Ah, my lady, my lady! This comes of your journey to 130
London. But now I'll have a frolic of my own, madam;
therefore pack up your trumpery this very night, for the
moment my horses are able to crawl, you and your brats
shall make a journey into the country again.

LADY WRONGHEAD.

Indeed, you are mistaken, Sir Francis. I shall not stir 135
out of town yet, I promise you.

SIR FRANCIS.

Not stir! Waunds, madam—

MANLY.

Hold, sir. If you'll give me leave a little, I fancy I shall
prevail with my lady to think better on't.

SIR FRANCIS.

Ah cousin, you are a friend indeed.   140

MANLY (*apart to my* Lady Wronghead).

Look you, madam, as to the favor you designed me, in
sending this spurious letter enclosed to my Lady Grace,
all the revenge I have taken is to have saved your son
and daughter from ruin. Now if you will take them
fairly and quietly into the country again, I will save 145
your ladyship from ruin.

LADY WRONGHEAD.

What do you mean, sir?

MANLY.

Why, Sir Francis shall never know what is in *this*

132. night] *02–3; 01 prints as*
catchword, but omits from text.

letter. [*Showing a second letter.*] Look upon it. How
it came into my hands you shall know at leisure.   150
LADY WRONGHEAD.

Ha, my billet-doux to the count—and an appointment
in it! I shall sink with confusion.
MANLY.

What shall I say to Sir Francis, madam?
LADY WRONGHEAD.

Dear sir, I am in such a trembling. Preserve my honor,
and I am all obedience.   155
MANLY.

Sir Francis, my lady is ready to receive your commands
for her journey, whenever you please to appoint it.
SIR FRANCIS.

Ah cousin, I doubt I am obliged to you for it.
MANLY.

Come, come, Sir Francis, take it as you find it. Obedience
in a wife is a good thing, though it were never so won-   160
derful. And now sir, we have nothing to do but to
dispose of this gentleman.
COUNT BASSET.

Mr. Manly! Sir! I hope you won't ruin me.
MANLY.

Did not you forge this note for five hundred pound, sir?
COUNT BASSET.

Sir, I see you know the world, and therefore I shall not 165
pretend to prevaricate. But it has hurt nobody yet,
sir. I beg you will not stigmatize me. Since you have
spoiled my fortune in one family, I hope you won't be
so cruel to a young fellow as to put it out of my power,
sir, to make it in another, sir.   170
MANLY.

Look you, sir, I have not much time to waste with you—
but if you expect mercy yourself, you must show it to
one you have been cruel to.

---

167. *stigmatize*] brand with infamy, both metaphorically and literally: a felon successfully pleading benefit of clergy on his first offense
would be burnt in the hand. Once branded he faced the death
penalty on a second conviction.

COUNT BASSET.

Cruel, sir?

MANLY.

Have not you ruined this young woman?   175

COUNT BASSET.

I, sir?

MANLY.

I know you have; therefore you can't blame her if, in
the fact you are charged with, she is a principal witness
against you. However, you have one, and one only
chance to get off with. Marry her this instant—and you 180
take off her evidence.

COUNT BASSET.

Dear sir—

MANLY.

No words, sir. A wife, or a mittimus.

COUNT BASSET.

Lord, sir, this is the most unmerciful mercy.

MANLY.

A private penance, or a public one. —Constable!   185

COUNT BASSET.

Hold, sir. Since you are pleased to give me my choice, I
will not make so ill a compliment to the lady as not to
give her the preference.

MANLY.

It must be done this minute, sir. The chaplain you
expected is still within call.   190

COUNT BASSET.

Well sir, since it must be so—come, spouse. I am not the
first of the fraternity that has run his head into one
noose, to keep it out of another.

MYRTILLA.

Come sir, don't repine. Marriage is, at worst, but playing
upon the square.   195

---

178. *fact*] crime.

180–181. *Marry . . . evidence*] since a wife cannot be called to give
evidence against her husband.

183. *mittimus*] a warrant issued by a Justice of the Peace, com-
mitting a person to prison to await trial.

195. *upon the square*] The phrase means both "honestly, without
fraud," and "on terms of equality with one another."

COUNT BASSET.

Aye, but the worst of the match, too, is the devil.

MANLY.

Well sir, to let you see it is not so bad as you think it:
as a reward for her honesty in detecting your practices,
instead of the forged bill you would have put upon
her, there's a real one of five hundred pound, to begin   200
a new honeymoon with.   *Gives it to* Myrtilla.

COUNT BASSET.

Sir, this is so generous an act—

MANLY.

No compliments, dear sir, I am not at leisure now to
receive them. Mr. Constable, will you be so good as to
wait upon this gentleman into the next room, and give   205
this lady in marriage to him?

CONSTABLE.

Sir, I'll do it faithfully.

COUNT BASSET.

Well, five hundred will serve to make a handsome push
with, however.

               Exeunt Count Basset, Myrtilla, *and* Constable.

SIR FRANCIS.

And that I may be sure my family's rid of him for-   210
ever—come my lady, let's even take our children along
with us, and be all witness of the ceremony.

Exeunt Sir Francis, Lady Wronghead, Miss Jenny *and* Squire
Richard.

MANLY.

Now, my lord, you may enter.

               Enter Lord *and* Lady Townly, *and* Lady Grace.

LORD TOWNLY.

So, sir, I give you joy of your negotiation.

MANLY.

You overheard it all, I presume?   215

202. an] *03*; a *01-2.*

---

196. *but the worst . . . devil*] The Count puns on *match* as marriage
and game. He gets the worst of it because he has lost the fruits of
his intrigue and gained a penniless ex-mistress.

LADY GRACE.

From first to last, sir.

LORD TOWNLY.

Never were knaves and fools better disposed of.

MANLY.

A sort of poetical justice, my lord, not much above the judgment of a modern comedy.

LORD TOWNLY.

To heighten that resemblance, I think, sister, there only 220
wants your rewarding the hero of the fable by naming
the day of his happiness.

LADY GRACE.

This day, tomorrow, every hour I hope of life to come,
will show I want not inclination to complete it.

MANLY.

Whatever I may want, madam, you will always find en- 225
deavors to deserve you.

LORD TOWNLY.

Then all are happy.

LADY TOWNLY.

Sister, I give you joy, consummate as the happiest pair
can boast.

> In you, methinks, as in a glass, I see   230
> The happiness that once advanced to me.
> So visible the bliss, so plain the way,
> How was it possible my sense could stray?
> But now, a convert, to this truth I come—
> That married happiness is never found from home.   235

[Exeunt.]

---

221. *fable*] the plot of the play.

EPILOGUE

Spoken by Mrs. Oldfield

Methinks I hear some powdered critics say,
"Damn it! this wife reformed has spoilt the play!
The coxcomb should have drawn her more in fashion,
Have gratified her softer inclination,
Have tipped her a gallant, and clinched the provocation." } 5
But there our bard stopped short: for 'twere uncivil
T'have made a modern belle, all o'er a devil.
He hoped, in honor of the sex, the age
Would bear one mended woman—on the stage.
    From whence, you see, by common sense's rules   10
Wives might be governed, were not husbands fools.
Whate'er by nature dames are prone to do,
They seldom stray, but when they govern you.
When the wild wife perceives her deary tame,
No wonder then she plays him all the game.   15
But men of sense meet rarely that disaster;
Women take pride, where merit is their master.
Nay, she that with a weak man wisely lives,
Will seem t'obey the due commands she gives.
Happy obedience is no more a wonder,   20
When men are men, and keep them kindly under.
But modern consorts are such high-bred creatures,
They think a husband's power degrades their features;
That nothing more proclaims a reigning beauty
Than that she never was reproached with duty;   25
And that the greatest blessing heav'n e'er sent,
Is in a spouse incurious, and content.
    To give such dames a different cast of thought
By calling home the mind, these scenes were wrought.
If with a hand too rude the task is done,   30
We hope the scheme by Lady Grace laid down
Will all such freedom with the sex atone;
That virtue there unsoiled by modish art,
Throws out attractions for a Manly's heart.

---

5. *tipped her*] given her, let her have (rogues' slang).
15. *plays . . . game*] cheats him in order to win.

You, you then, ladies, whose unquestioned lives   35
Give you the foremost fame of happy wives,
Protect, for its attempt, this helpless play,
Nor leave it to the vulgar taste a prey;
Appear the frequent champions of its cause,
Direct the crowd, and give yourselves applause.   40

Appendix

Chronology

Approximate dates are indicated by *. Dates for plays are those on which they were first made public, either on stage or in print.

Political and Literary Events

Lives and Major Works of Vanbrugh and Cibber

1631
Death of Donne.
John Dryden born.

1633
Samuel Pepys born.

1635
Sir George Etherege born.*

1640
Aphra Behn born.*

1641
William Wycherley born.*

1642
First Civil War began (ended 1646).
Theaters closed by Parliament.
Thomas Shadwell born.*

1648
Second Civil War.
Nathaniel Lee born.*

1649
Execution of Charles I.

1650
Jeremy Collier born.

1651
Hobbes's *Leviathan* published.

1652
First Dutch War began (ended 1654).

Thomas Otway born.

1656

D'Avenant's *THE SIEGE OF RHODES* performed at Rutland House.

1657

John Dennis born.

1658

Death of Oliver Cromwell.
D'Avenant's *THE CRUELTY OF THE SPANIARDS IN PERU* performed at the Cockpit.

1660

Restoration of Charles II.
Theatrical patents granted to Thomas Killigrew and Sir William D'Avenant, authorizing them to form, respectively, the King's and the Duke of York's Companies.
Pepys began his diary.

1661

Cowley's *THE CUTTER OF COLEMAN STREET*.
D'Avenant's *THE SIEGE OF RHODES* (expanded to two parts).

1662

Charter granted to the Royal Society.

1663

Dryden's *THE WILD GALLANT*.
Tuke's *THE ADVENTURES OF FIVE HOURS*.

1664

Dryden's *THE RIVAL LADIES*.
Dryden and Howard's *THE INDIAN QUEEN*.
Etherege's *THE COMICAL REVENGE*.

Vanbrugh born, in London (christened January 24).

1665

Second Dutch War began (ended 1667).

Great Plague.
Dryden's *THE INDIAN EM-
PEROR.*
Orrery's *MUSTAPHA.*

1666
Fire of London.
Death of James Shirley.

1667
Jonathan Swift born.
Milton's *Paradise Lost* published.
Sprat's *The History of the Royal
Society* published.
Dryden's *SECRET LOVE.*

1668
Death of D'Avenant.
Dryden made Poet Laureate.
Dryden's *An Essay of Dramatic
Poesy* published.
Shadwell's *THE SULLEN LOV-
ERS.*
Etherege's *SHE WOULD IF SHE
COULD.*

1669
Pepys terminated his diary.
Susanna Centlivre born.

1670
William Congreve born.
Dryden's *THE CONQUEST OF
GRANADA,* Part I.

1671
Dorset Garden Theatre (Duke's   Cibber born, in London, Novem-
Company) opened.   ber 6.
Milton's *Paradise Regained* and
Samson Agonistes published.
Dryden's *THE CONQUEST OF
GRANADA,* Part II.
THE REHEARSAL, by the Duke
of Buckingham and others.
Wycherley's *LOVE IN A WOOD.*

1672
Third Dutch War began (ended
1674).

Joseph Addison born.
Richard Steele born.
Dryden's *MARRIAGE A LA MODE.*

1674
New Drury Lane Theatre (King's Company) opened.
Death of Milton.
Nicholas Rowe born.
Thomas Rymer's *Reflections on Aristotle's Treatise of Poesy* (translation of Rapin) published.

1675
Dryden's *AURENG-ZEBE.*
Wycherley's *THE COUNTRY WIFE.*

1676
Etherege's *THE MAN OF MODE.*
Otway's *DON CARLOS.*
Shadwell's *THE VIRTUOSO.*
Wycherley's *THE PLAIN DEALER.*

1677
Rymer's *Tragedies of the Last Age Considered* published.
Aphra Behn's *THE ROVER.*
Dryden's *ALL FOR LOVE.*
Lee's *THE RIVAL QUEENS.*

1678
Popish Plot.
George Farquhar born.
Bunyan's *Pilgrim's Progress* (Part I) published.

1679
Exclusion Bill introduced.
Death of Thomas Hobbes.
Death of Roger Boyle, Earl of Orrery.
Charles Johnson born.

1680
Death of Samuel Butler.

Death of John Wilmot, Earl of
Rochester.
Dryden's *THE SPANISH FRIAR.*
Lee's *LUCIUS JUNIUS BRUTUS.*
Otway's *THE ORPHAN.*

1681
Charles II dissolved Parliament at
Oxford.
Dryden's *Absalom and Achitophel*
published.
Tate's adaptation of *KING LEAR.*

1682
The King's and the Duke of
York's Companies merged into the
United Company.
Dryden's *The Medal, MacFleck-
noe,* and *Religio Laici* published.
Otway's *VENICE PRESERVED.*

1683
Rye House Plot.
Death of Thomas Killigrew.
Crowne's *CITY POLITIQUES.*

1685
Death of Charles II; accession of
James II.
Revocation of the Edict of Nantes.
The Duke of Monmouth's Rebel-
lion.
Death of Otway.
John Gay born.
Crowne's *SIR COURTLY NICE.*
Dryden's *ALBION AND AL-
BANIUS.*

1686

Vanbrugh commissioned in Lord
Huntingdon's regiment.

1687
Death of the Duke of Bucking-
ham.
Dryden's *The Hind and the
Panther* published.
Newton's *Principia* published.

1688
The Revolution.
Alexander Pope born.
Shadwell's THE SQUIRE OF AL-
SATIA.

Vanbrugh arrested and impri-
soned in France.

1689
The War of the League of Augs-
burg began (ended 1697).
Toleration Act.
Death of Aphra Behn.
Shadwell made Poet Laureate.
Dryden's DON SEBASTIAN.
Shadwell's BURY FAIR.

1690
Battle of the Boyne.
Locke's Two Treatises of Govern-
ment and An Essay Concerning
Human Understanding published.

Cibber began his stage career at
Drury Lane.

1691
Death of Etherege.*
Langbaine's An Account of the
English Dramatic Poets published.

1692
Death of Lee.
Death of Shadwell.
Tate made Poet Laureate.

Vanbrugh released from Bastille;
returned to England, November.

1693
George Lillo born.*
Rymer's A Short View of Tragedy
published.
Congreve's THE OLD BACHE-
LOR.

Cibber married Katherine Shore.

1694
Death of Queen Mary.
Southerne's THE FATAL MAR-
RIAGE.

1695
Group of actors led by Thomas
Betterton left Drury Lane and
established a new company at
Lincoln's Inn Fields.
Congreve's LOVE FOR LOVE.
Southerne's OROONOKO.

1696

Cibber's *LOVE'S LAST SHIFT*
(Drury Lane, January).
Vanbrugh's *THE RELAPSE*
(Drury Lane, November 21).

1697

Treaty of Ryswick ended the War of the League of Augsburg.
Charles Macklin born.
Congreve's *THE MOURNING BRIDE*.

Vanbrugh's *THE PROVOKED WIFE* (Lincoln's Inn Fields, April).

1698

Collier controversy started with the publication of *A Short View of the Immorality and Profaneness of the English Stage*.

Vanbrugh published *A Short Vindication of "The Relapse" and "The Provoked Wife" from Immorality and Profaneness*.
Vanbrugh's *THE COUNTRY HOUSE* (Drury Lane, January).

1699

Farquhar's *THE CONSTANT COUPLE*.

Vanbrugh appointed architect of Castle Howard, Yorkshire.

1700

Death of Dryden.
Blackmore's *Satire against Wit* published.
Congreve's *THE WAY OF THE WORLD*.

1701

Act of Settlement.
War of the Spanish Succession began (ended 1713).
Death of James II.
Rowe's *TAMERLANE*.
Steele's *THE FUNERAL*.

1702

Death of William III; accession of Anne.
The Daily Courant began publication.

Vanbrugh's *THE FALSE FRIEND* (Drury Lane, February).
Cibber's *SHE WOULD AND SHE WOULD NOT* (Drury Lane, November 26).

1703

Death of Samuel Pepys.
Rowe's *THE FAIR PENITENT*.

1704

Capture of Gibraltar; Battle of Blenheim.
Defoe's *The Review* began publication (1704–1713).
Swift's *A Tale of a Tub* and *The Battle of the Books* published.

Cibber's *THE CARELESS HUS-BAND* (Drury Lane, December 7).

1705

Steele's *THE TENDER HUS-BAND.*

Opening of Queen's Theatre, Haymarket (April 9), designed and managed by Vanbrugh.
Vanbrugh appointed Surveyor for the building of Blenheim Palace (June).
Vanbrugh's *THE CONFEDER-ACY* (Haymarket, October 30), and *THE MISTAKE* (Haymarket, December 27).

1706

Battle of Ramillies.
Farquhar's *THE RECRUITING OFFICER.*

1707

Union of Scotland and England.
Death of Farquhar.
Henry Fielding born.
Farquhar's *THE BEAUX' STRATAGEM.*

Cibber's *THE LADY'S LAST STAKE* (Haymarket, December 13).

1708

Downes's *Roscius Anglicanus* published.

1709

Samuel Johnson born.
Rowe's edition of Shakespeare published.
The Tatler began publication (1709–1711).
Centlivre's *THE BUSY BODY.*

1711

Shaftesbury's *Characteristics* published.
The Spectator began publication

Cibber, Wilks, and Doggett established as managers of the Drury Lane Theatre.

(1711–1712).
Pope's *An Essay on Criticism* published.

1713
Treaty of Utrecht ended the War of the Spanish Succession.
Addison's *CATO*.

1714
Death of Anne; accession of George I.

Vanbrugh knighted.

Steele became Governor of Drury Lane.
John Rich assumed management of Lincoln's Inn Fields.
Centlivre's *THE WONDER: A WOMAN KEEPS A SECRET*.
Rowe's *JANE SHORE*.

1715
Jacobite Rebellion.
Death of Tate.
Rowe made Poet Laureate.
Death of Wycherley.

1716
Addison's *THE DRUMMER*.

Vanbrugh appointed architect for Greenwich Hospital.

1717
David Garrick born.
Gay, Pope, and Arbuthnot's *THREE HOURS AFTER MARRIAGE*.

Cibber's *THE NON-JUROR* (Drury Lane, December 6).

1718
Death of Rowe.
Centlivre's *A BOLD STROKE FOR A WIFE*.

1719
Death of Addison.
Defoe's *Robinson Crusoe* published.

Vanbrugh married Henrietta Yarborough.

Young's *BUSIRIS, KING OF EGYPT*.

1720
South Sea Bubble.
Samuel Foote born.

Steele suspended from the Governorship of Drury Lane (restored 1721).

Little Theatre in the Haymarket opened.

Steele's *The Theatre* (periodical) published.

Hughes's *THE SIEGE OF DAMASCUS.*

1721
Walpole became first Minister.

1722
Steele's *THE CONSCIOUS LOVERS.*

1723
Death of Susanna Centlivre.
Death of D'Urfey.

1725
Pope's edition of Shakespeare published.

1726
Death of Jeremy Collier.
Law's *Unlawfulness of Stage Entertainments* published.
Swift's *Gulliver's Travels* published.

Death of Vanbrugh, March 26.

1727
Death of George I; accession of George II.
Death of Sir Isaac Newton.
Arthur Murphy born.

1728
Pope's *The Dunciad* (first version) published.
Gay's *THE BEGGAR'S OPERA.*

THE PROVOKED HUSBAND (Drury Lane, January 10).

1729
Goodman's Fields Theatre opened.
Death of Congreve.
Death of Steele.
Edmund Burke born.

1730
Oliver Goldsmith born.

Cibber appointed Poet Laureate.

Thomson's *The Seasons* published.
Fielding's *THE AUTHOR'S FARCE.*
Fielding's *TOM THUMB* (revised as *THE TRAGEDY OF TRAGEDIES*, 1731).

1731
Death of Defoe.
Fielding's *THE GRUB-STREET OPERA.*
Lillo's *THE LONDON MERCHANT.*

1732
Covent Garden Theatre opened.
Death of Gay.
George Colman the elder born.
Fielding's *THE COVENT GARDEN TRAGEDY.*
Fielding's *THE MODERN HUSBAND.*
Charles Johnson's *CAELIA.*

1733
Pope's *An Essay on Man* (Epistle I–III) published (Epistle IV, 1734).

Cibber retired from the stage.

1734
Death of Dennis.
The Prompter began publication (1734–1736).
Theobald's edition of Shakespeare published.
Fielding's *DON QUIXOTE IN ENGLAND.*

1736
Fielding led the "Great Mogul's Company of Comedians" at the Little Theatre in the Haymarket (1736–1737).
Fielding's *PASQUIN.*
Lillo's *FATAL CURIOSITY.*

1737
The Stage Licensing Act.
Dodsley's *THE KING AND THE MILLER OF MANSFIELD.*

Fielding's *THE HISTORICAL REGISTER FOR 1736.*

1738

Johnson's *London* published.

Pope's *One Thousand Seven Hundred and Thirty-Eight* published.

Thomson's *AGAMEMNON.*

1739

War with Spain began.

Death of Lillo.

Hugh Kelly born.

Fielding's *The Champion* began publication (1739–1741).

Johnson's *Complete Vindication of Licensers of the Stage,* an ironical criticism of the Licensing Act, published after Brooke's *GUSTAVUS VASA* was denied a license.

1740

War of the Austrian Succession began (ended 1748).

James Boswell born.

Richardson's *Pamela* published.

Garrick's *LETHE.*

Thomson and Mallet's *ALFRED.*

Apology for the Life of Colley Cibber published.

1741

Edmond Malone born.

Garrick began acting.

Fielding's *Shamela* published.

Garrick's *THE LYING VALET.*

1742

Walpole resigned his offices.

Fielding's *Joseph Andrews* published.

Pope's *New Dunciad* (Book IV of *The Dunciad*) published.

Young's *The Complaint, or Night Thoughts* published (additional parts published each year until 1745).

First of Cibber's three *Letters to Mr. Pope* published.

1743

Death of Henry Carey.

Fielding's *Miscellanies* published.

Cibber enthroned as hero of Pope's revised *Dunciad.*

1744
Death of Pope.
Death of Theobald.
Dodsley's *A Select Collection of Old Plays* published.
Johnson's *Life of Mr. Richard Savage* published.

1745
Jacobite Rebellion.
Death of Swift.
Thomas Holcroft born.
Johnson's *Observations on Macbeth* published.
Thomson's *TANCRED AND SIGISMUNDA*.

Cibber's *PAPAL TYRANNY* (Covent Garden, February 15).

1746
Death of Southerne.
Collins's *Odes* published.

1747
Garrick entered the management of Drury Lane Theatre.
Johnson's *Prologue Spoken by Mr. Garrick at the Opening of the Theatre in Drury Lane, 1747.*
Warburton's edition of Shakespeare published.
Garrick's *MISS IN HER TEENS*.

1748
Treaty of Aix-la-Chapelle ended the War of the Austrian Succession.
Death of Thomson.
Hume's *Philosophical Essays Concerning Human Understanding* published.
Richardson's *Clarissa* published.
Smollett's *Roderick Random* published.

1749
Death of Ambrose Philips.
Bolingbroke's *Idea of a Patriot King* published.

Chetwood's *A General History of the Stage* published.

Fielding's *Tom Jones* published.

Johnson's *The Vanity of Human Wishes* published.

Hill's *MEROPE* (adaptation of Voltaire).

Johnson's *IRENE*.

1750

Death of Aaron Hill.

Johnson's *The Rambler* began publication (1750–1752).

1751

Death of Bolingbroke.

Richard Brinsley Sheridan born.

Gray's *An Elegy Wrote in a Country Churchyard* published.

Smollett's *Peregrine Pickle* published.

1752

Fielding's *Amelia* published.

Fielding's *The Covent Garden Journal* published.

Mason's *ELFRIDA* published.

1753

Death of Bishop Berkeley.

Elizabeth Inchbald born.

Foote's *THE ENGLISHMAN IN PARIS*.

Moore's *THE GAMESTER*.

Young's *THE BROTHERS*.

1754

Death of Fielding.

Richardson's *Sir Charles Grandison* published.

Whitehead's *CREUSA, QUEEN OF ATHENS*.

1755

Fielding's *Journal of a Voyage to Lisbon* published.

Johnson's *A Dictionary of the English Language* published.

1756
Seven Years War began.
William Godwin born.
Burke's *A Philosophical Enquiry into . . . the Sublime and Beautiful* published.
First part of Joseph Warton's *Essay on . . . Pope* published (second part, 1782).
Murphy's *THE APPRENTICE.*

1757
Battle of Plassey (India).
Death of Moore.
William Blake born.
Gray's *Odes* published.

Death of Cibber, December 11.